LEARNING CURVE

LEARNING CURVE

The Remarkable Story of
Student Rugby League

Scratching Shed Publishing Ltd

First published by Scratching Shed Publishing Ltd in 2013
Registered in England & Wales No. 6588772.
Registered office:
47 Street Lane, Leeds, West Yorkshire. LS8 1AP

www.scratchingshedpublishing.co.uk

ISBN 978-0956804389

Unless stated otherwise, all photographs are from the
personal collection of Andrew Cudbertson

Cover photograph: Oxford v Cambridge, 1995.

Back cover photograph: Leeds University v Liverpool University on
Leigh Rec, Widnes. First ever inter-university match, 15 March 1968.

A catalogue record for this book is available from the British Library.

Typeset in Papyrus and Palatino

Manufactured in the UK by LPPS Ltd,
Wellingborough, Northants, NN8 3PJ

Dedicated to the memory of Cec Thompson
and Phil Melling, two of the great pioneers

Sunday Mirror

Mark Lane
Corporation Street
Manchester 4

telegrams: Sunmirror Manchester 4
telephone: DEAnsgate 3444
extension:

The Daily Mirror Newspapers Limited

*Queens Hotel.
Leeds
Dec 11/67.*

Dear Sir,

Thank you for your letter. I was glad to hear from you for I had intended ringing Ces Thompson but had lost his phone number. I did write a note in my column on your club and this appeared in Lancashire and Cumberland. I shall be happy to come to give a show for you in the New Year, I shall require a 16mm projector with necessary screen etc. I would like to speak to the man who would handle this before I finalise details. Let me have your proposed dates and I will make arrangements to see your projectionist. Advise whether lunchtime or evening. The show can be timed for duration to suit your requirements.

I have been delighted to hear of your progress from one or two sources. Keep up the good work.

Please give my regards to Ces Thompson and explain my regret and reason for not ringing him.

With kind regards,
Sincerely.

Eddie Waring.

Registered Office: 33 Holborn London EC1

Sunday Mirror

The Daily Mirror Newspapers Limited

Mark Lane
Corporation Street
Manchester 4

telegrams: Sunmirror Manchester 4
telephone: DEAnsgate 3444
extension:

Queens Hotel. Leeds.
Jany 11th.68.

Dear Mr Cudbertson.

Apropos my show for you. Would Thurs Feb 8th be as suitable for you as the 6th. The reason for this is the fact that the 1st rnd R.L. cup date is Feb 3rd. Any draw would take place either on the 6th or the 7th. If the 6th I might be called upon to cover it for Sportsview which might mean my personal absence although I would get someone to take over. We might make the drew for the 2nd round on the 5th so suggest that week would be better on the 8th. Otherwise I could take the 13th which is on a Tuesday on my return from Paris. Please let me have your views.

Yours Sincerely.

Registered Office: 33 Holborn London EC1

Star support: Letters to Leeds University RLFC from Eddie Waring

Contents

Contents (cont)

Foreword One

■

David Oxley CBE

Former chief executive, Rugby Football League,
president and former chairman, Student Rugby League

As the current president and, for many years, the proud chairman of the Student Rugby League, I was delighted when Dave Hadfield agreed to take up the commission to produce the official history of the SRL.

Dave is a superb writer, justly held in the highest regard throughout the rugby league world. What is more, he has always shown a keen and committed interest in the progress of student rugby league, from the mid-60s when it was pioneered by visionaries such as Andrew Cudbertson and Cec Thompson.

Despite having to combat early prejudice and some apathy, the student game is now well established as an important member of the rugby league family, greatly enjoyed alike by those who wish to play purely for fun and those who possess the talent and commitment to aspire to the highest level of representative and international football.

Apart from producing players for Super League, Championship and top amateur clubs, it has been the entry point for countless coaches, development officers and administrators.

The positive influence of former student players going out into the wider world with rugby league in their hearts and prospering in industry, business, commerce, government office, the armed services and parliament is now fully recognised and understood throughout the game.

This is an inspiring story and I can think of no-one better able to celebrate it than Dave Hadfield.

His beautifully written history will interest, inform, enlighten and delight students, scholars, historians and all true aficionados of the great game.

David Oxley CBE,
January 2013

Foreword Two

■

Brian Carney
Ex_Ireland Students
Plus Gateshead, Hull, Wigan, Warrington & GB & Ireland

It's good to see an area of the game that sometimes remains hidden receive such a thorough documenting. I have said before that it is a demographic the game needs to continue to nurture, as student league has the potential to be one of the game's greatest resources.

I finished four years of university without really knowing about rugby league.

In my final summer Brian Corrigan persuaded me to give it a try, with the promise of an international tournament in Scotland as the carrot. I made the squad for that Four Nations and had one of the most enjoyable sporting experiences ever.

Coached by Liam Horrigan and the legendary Irish development officer, Nigel Johnson, I enjoyed every minute - except losing to England - meeting so many second generation Irish from areas like Hull, Wigan and St Helens, who were bursting with pride at the opportunity to pull on the green jersey.

One of my team-mates, Sasch Brook, had sorted himself an office job at the soon-to-be Super League Gateshead Thunder. Sasch brought a video of the tournament to show to Shane Richardson, the chief executive. Shane asked for my details and the rest, as they say, is history.

Good luck to student rugby league. Brian, Nigel, Sasch and the student game all came together to give me a wonderful chapter in my life.

Brian Carney,
January 2013

Introduction:
A Degree of Separation

First of all, a confession. I never played student rugby league.

Oh yes, I stretched out my student days for as long as humanly possible. I had a gap year before they were invented, which I spent learning a few things whilst working as a hospital porter and hitch-hiking around Europe.

After that I did the then standard four years at Keele - a very good system for producing crash-hot *University Challenge* teams - and one year learning, in theory, to be a journalist in Cardiff.

'Avoid long words, like marmalade and corrugated.' That's the one lesson I remember from there; but, one way or another, I had my money's worth from the then bounteous British tax-payer.

All the time I was a student, I was playing and watching rugby league when I had the chance, but never quite putting the two - the student and the rugby league - together. That was because, coming at it from my direction, you had to make a choice between rugby league and an education - or four years at a holiday camp with occasional exams.

For many, the choice was effectively made even before that. My school-mates from Leigh, for instance, had played league at primary school. The only way to carry on after that was to fail your 11-plus. By the time you went to university or college, you were used to the idea that rugby league was something you did outside the education system, not within it.

So I did what most of us did and settled for playing rugby union. In my case, it was a curious, U-shaped career. Big and keen when I arrived, I went straight into the first XV and spent two seasons working my way downwards.

The trouble was that it was just too boring. There were, from memory, three of us with league roots, the other two from Barrow and Normanton respectively, who realised this.

Occasionally, we would exchange guilty looks, as if to say: 'What are we doing messing about with this?'

There was also the danger of giving yourself away by counting heads before games and saying: 'That's 13, we've got a team.'

There was a bit of pleasure to be had from the thought that, under the draconian amateurism rules of the time, I had not only professionalised anyone I'd played with, but anyone I'd played against as well. It was like being the carrier of some deadly disease, but marginally more fun.

In the end, I ran out of motivation so completely that I failed to get up in time for a 7.30 kick-off. It was time to knock it on the head, although I had a weird Indian summer in my final year, played a couple of games and finished up where I started, trundling around and grumbling to myself in the first XV.

What I should have done, of course, was play the bold pioneer and get a league team going. But that would have seemed like far too much effort. Besides, there was no guarantee of raising a team, just the certainty of being black-balled from the drinking games of your erstwhile team-mates.

It could all have been different if I had ever realised that my American Literature tutor, Phil Melling, was a Wiganer and a rugby league nut, who would go on to establish the game at student level in South Wales. I didn't really go to enough tutorials to make the connection. Besides, he was a Hemingway buff and I was more of a Kurt Vonnegut man.

It might have been different, as well, if I'd known that there were others elsewhere who were showing some energy and enterprise. There were stirrings at Leeds, at Liverpool, at Sheffield - even some of my old school team were involved.

My excuse is that I was still recovering from the strain of A-levels; I know, not very convincing, is it? It's on a par with my explanation to another tutor for a piece of work left undone: Quite frankly, I couldn't be bothered. And this, remember, was well before the advent of daytime television. What I would have been like with that added to the equation, heaven only knows.

A hippy haven like Keele was not exactly a bastion of competitive sport. It wasn't a bastion of competitive anything. I turned down a place in the *University Challenge* team - it was a bad year - because I thought it was uncool. I wouldn't say I've regretted that decision; I've just woken up every morning since and thought: 'What a wanker!'

The prevailing attitude to sport is best summed up by a team picture from an end-of-term kickabout that I have just rediscovered. Most members of my F Block side are holding spliffs the size and shape of prize-winning parsnips. I have vague recollections of scoring a penalty past Gordon Banks; this admittedly after he lost an eye in a car-crash (and I put it on his blind side).

As for traditional local rivalries, we didn't really have any, although there was talk of a suicide pact with Madeley Teachers' College, a few miles away down country lanes.

That, I think, establishes my credentials - or lack of them - for the task ahead. Late in the day, I know, but perhaps I can make my contribution now, rather than on a muddy field in North Staffordshire 40 years ago.

Rugby league doesn't have the longest history amongst sports, but it does have arguably the most fascinating. My theory is that this is because it is basically the story of getting it into places where it wasn't meant to be. It's about the breaking down of barriers, be they geographic, cultural, social or educational.

The barricade that tumbled down when rugby league started to be played in universities and colleges did a lot of collateral damage. As a first breakthrough, it pointed the way forward at many other levels - the police, the armed forces and the civil service, to name a few.

Student rugby league has been an essential part of geographic and social expansion of the code over the last four decades.

Not only do old slackers like me have no excuse any more, but young people from way outside the traditional heartlands have been able to get a taste for the code - and take that interest with them to wherever they go next.

And the social and cultural mix of rugby league clubs - large and small - has changed. Quite apart from the ones that owe their very existence to the student game, it is not unusual, from Wigan down to the smallest village club in the Pennine League, to find a few lads with degrees who were able to maintain their rugby league careers - or even to discover the game - during their student days.

I once played in a front row where we had seven degrees between us. Not much in the way of rugby intelligence - that mysterious quality which Gareth Hock has, but Prof Stephen Hawking doesn't - nor, indeed, common sense, but seven degrees none the less. It must prove something and, if

I could get a research grant for three years, I might be able to tell you what.

Just after I took on this project, I went to the SRL final at Headingley between Leeds Met and Loughborough. Calling in a café for a cup of coffee before the match, I got talking to a man from Leigh, whose son was playing for Leeds. Unlike many of my contemporaries, he had been able to play his game of choice throughout his university days and was now weighing up whether he could combine Championship rugby with a full-time job. His ability has not been lost to a sport that needs greater quantity and quality of players - and what's more he was man of the match.

When Niel Wood and the Student Rugby League approached me about this venture, I delayed because I didn't want to write a conventional, chronological history. Eventually, they convinced me that it wasn't what they wanted either. What you have here, therefore, is more of a series of linked essays - or what yet another of my lecturers would have called 'a typical load of old flannel.'

For what merit and value it does have, I need to thank the array of people who have shared their experiences with me. They are all mentioned in the text, but I must award first-class Honours to Andrew Cudbertson, a man for whom the term pioneer is inadequate and whose book it is as much as it is mine; to Tracey O'Mara at the SRL; to Brian Carney and David Oxley for the forewords; to Phil, Tony and Ros at Scratching Shed; and to Niel Wood, the driving force behind the project, for confirming another of my theories - namely that every good team, educated or uneducated, needs at least one player whose name is spelt wrongly.

He once phoned me from a clearing in a birch wood on the banks of the Volga - to which he had been directed by an old woman in two raincoats, herding goats - to tell me I really ought to have gone on that particular student tour to

Kazan. When I heard the balalaikas in the background, I had to agree with him.

The chance to write an account of the last 45 years enables me to make up some lost time.

It has been a task that has expanded as it has gone on and which has led me in directions I never expected. Lift one stone and there beneath it are a couple more, so, if your particular triumphs and struggles are under one that has so far been left unturned, my apologies.

Dave Hadfield,
January 2013

1. Archaeology:
Exhuming the Bones of Portsmouth Poly

On November 18, 1966, a five-paragraph story appeared in the *Rugby Leaguer*, then the only weekly publication covering the game.

Tucked in among the regular notes from Keighley and Barrow, below the personal ads for two marriage bureaux - good sense of humour and a lively interest in rugby league essential, you would have thought - it bracketed together three unconnected developments in the amateur game.

There was the news that the UGB - United Glass Blowers - club in St Helens was re-forming after lapsing for a year. Nearby, the Merseyside Sea Cadets were setting up a league.

The officer in charge of the area, Lt Cmdr A.E. Stanton, was quoted as saying: 'There is no better game for the inculcation of team spirit and to gain the highest physical fitness and that is what we want.'

No such claim was made on behalf of the third element

of this disparate trio, but it did make the intro, which ran thus: 'A Rugby League team has been formed at Portsmouth College of Technology. One of the organisers, Mr Peter D. Tate, a Bradford Northern supporter, has asked for information about any amateur clubs willing to play in the South. His address is 20, Exeter Road, Southsea, Hants.'

There are a surprising number of Peter Tates in the Bradford telephone directory; I should know, because I've spoken to most of them. And that was making the assumption that this forgotten pioneer finished up back in his home city.

At least one source assured me that he had emigrated to Canada. Not quite, but he did live in Jamaica for a while. It was that connection that produced the vital clue - a picture from a few years back on the internet, showing a Peter Tate alongside Steven Pryce of the Jamaican RL. Too much of a coincidence. Another contact came up with a phone number at the Bradford Council for Voluntary Service and, sure enough, there he was, a man as we shall see, who blazed a trail for rugby league more than once.

The right Peter Tate is waiting for me at a bus stop on Manchester Road, the route between Bradford city centre and Odsal that used to boast, he remembers from his youth, 26 pubs. He is now a short, stocky man in his 60s, still recognisably built like an old-school hooker. We take the short walk to his house, apparently going through the estate known locally as 'Beirut'. Sitting in the sunshine in his back garden, he tells me the story.

Peter went to what was then Portsmouth College of Technology in 1966 to study Geography. Within a few weeks he decided that what it needed was a rugby league team, despite it being as far south as you could go without attempting to colonise the Isle of Wight and two or three hours from the closest opposition.

'I looked at the northern lads there, half-pissed on lousy ale, and wondered what we could do to preserve and reclaim our culture,' he recalls, tongue slightly in cheek. Unlike some of the pioneers who figure in this story, Tate cheerfully admits to having an agenda. 'For me, it's all tied in with my politics. I've always been on the left, on the side of the disadvantaged. It's a good fit with rugby league.'

He managed to find enough like-minded northerners to form the nucleus of a side. More surprisingly, he found a number of Welsh students keen to have a go. Inevitably, that involved a little subterfuge and deception, with the Welsh rugby union players appearing under assumed names.

'That first season, we had a Terry Price, a Berwyn Jones and a Vince Karalius,' Tate says.

Training was on the Common at Southsea, looking across the Solent, and a small grant from the Students' Union, whose president was one of the league players, bought a couple of balls. For their match kit, the new club was indebted to Castleford, who responded to an appeal by donating the previous season's shirts. Tate had Johnny Ward's number nine, whilst his mate from Keighley, Dave Crutchley, had the star prize of Malcolm Reilly's number 13 loose forward jumper.

'They were a bit faded, but they still felt pretty good,' Tate says. 'There was some opposition. The rugby union club tried to stop us getting a pitch. But we just said "You can't do that. It's 1966; you can't stop people playing the game they want to".'

By the time they did so competitively, it was 1967 and it involved a journey to Hackney Marshes to play a scratch London side. Home games were played at Eastern Road playing fields in Portsmouth and, the following season, the club was part of the rebirth of a Southern Amateur League, which had been defunct since the mid-50s.

By the time Tate finished his three-year course in 1969, Portsmouth had a well-established team playing in a reasonably stable competition.

Portsmouth's finest hour came when they reached the final of the John Player-sponsored Southern League Cup in 1972, playing Hillingdon at Watford, and being beaten by a late, late drop goal.

'They were hanging on at 11-11 and Hillingdon were penning them back on their own line. From a play-the-ball, the acting half-back threw out a long pass to the Hillingdon full-back,' remembers the referee that day, Peter Wilson. 'Maybe I shouldn't admit this even after all this time, but since I was back on the try-line and my two touch judges were in the corners, none of us had the faintest idea of whether the drop goal attempt was successful. I just had to go on the reaction of the Hillingdon full-back, who leapt in the air in triumph.

'So I gave a goal and, as nobody in the Portsmouth team argued the point, I trusted my guess was right.

'It was only when we all went up to receive our medals from Clive Sullivan - the referee is always at the back, as you know - that somebody rushed towards the front of the stand and took a swing and yelled: "You're a fucking disgrace to the game, Wilson." Maybe it was because I had sent him off in the semi-final, which meant he was banned from the Final, I don't know.'

The referee, then fighting the good fight for rugby league in Corby, was the same Peter Wilson who became the long-serving correspondent to the *Daily Star*. Now semi-retired on Walney Island, near Barrow, he writes western novels, which have a mysterious tendency to feature places and characters with familiar rugby league names, such as a ghost town called Ganson and a Sheriff Jim Gannon. (Now he would really clean up that one-horse town.)

Peter Tate had long moved on by then, although bizarrely there was a P. Tate playing for Hillingdon that day.

The Portsmouth scrum-half was Peter Dawson, who now lives in Sydney and runs a website called Rugby Sidestep Central, devoted, as you might guess, to the magic of the sidestep. On it, he reflects on his career, including turning out for the Polytechnic, although without the inconvenience of being a student there. Despite being new to rugby league, he was offered trials by Warrington and Keighley and actually played one for the latter.

'They didn't want me because I was too small and I'm sure they were right in my case.' He remembers one of the side's Welsh 'ringers', Dave Davies, who worked at Ferrantis: 'What a fantastic player he was.'

The match programme for that final says: 'It may come as a surprise to read that Portsmouth Polytechnic were one of the very first teams to play in the South. In fact, they travelled to Hackney Marshes to meet the London RL Association (as it then was) as far back as 1967, before club differentiation had taken place in the metropolis.

'The moving spirit in that venture was Peter Tate and the club he helped to found has been a credit to southern rugby since then. As with all the 'academic' sides, playing strength fluctuates from year to year and within the season. Today's match, for example, is perilously close to the beginning of the examination season. If a Poly man muffs an easy chance, remember he may have other things on his mind!'

Elsewhere in the programme, there is an insight into southern rugby league's long-term strategy.

'Another highly promising area of development is the educational world,' wrote Thamesman. 'The game is already firmly established in higher education as Portsmouth Polytechnic will demonstrate today. A campaign to spread the game further in southern colleges and universities is now being planned. Associated with this is a scheme to strengthen links with the SRL by forming a team to cater for graduates, particularly those coming down from the north who want to maintain their old friendships. It should be emphasised, though, that membership will be open; the organisers do not wish to form a 'snob' club!'

It could have been a mission statement, thirty-odd years later, for the London Skolars.

Although Peter Tate was only at Sheffield for a year, it was long enough for him to launch the game there and it was he who asked Fred Lindop to coach the side. Sheffield are still thriving, but Portsmouth fizzled out in the mid-70s. On the website of what is now the University of Portsmouth, the rugby union club is described as the biggest of their sporting clubs. There is no mention of rugby league or the institution's supporting role in its history.

All the same, Tate cannot fail to reflect his pleasure, as we sit in one of the surviving pubs on Manchester Road with his next-door neighbour Naz, in the way the student game has expanded in the years since he set the ball rolling on the Hampshire coast.

"There is some satisfaction in that,' he says. 'I'm an initiator. I like to get things started.'

That was the case after his student days, when he was teaching geography in Dewsbury, and when he was involved in relaunching rugby league in Batley and Dewsbury schools, twice taking them to Wembley - once as ball boys, once to play in the curtain-raiser. Then there's his connection with the game in Jamaica, where he might finish up living and working for part of the year, and his continuing support for the Bradford Bulls. He has done his bit for his game - and then some.

In his home city now, he is a voice for the barrier-breaking power of sport. He takes delight, for instance, that the leading local crown-green bowler in the area is a Muslim with a luxuriant beard.

But here's the rub; rugby league pioneer as he undoubtedly was, he might not have been the first. Back in the dusty files there are veiled references to a team at Staffordshire College of Technology, travelling to London to play Southern opposition. They undoubtedly existed at some moment in time, but they do not appear to have joined a league and they did not last.

An even more tenuous claim to trail-blazing status belongs to the London School of Economics. Peter Reed, who was later involved in launching the game at Reading University, recalls playing informal, 'pick-up' matches in Regents Park in the mid-50s. 'It started with a challenge between me, from Featherstone, and my friend, from Wakefield. We had no kit, posts or pitch-markings, so you can't call them organised games,' he says now. They did, however, cause quite a stir with passers-by, some of whom were keen enough to have a try. It's a slender thread, but a thread all the same.

If we really want to delve back into the age of myths and legends, there is evidence of a game at Oxford in 1934, which figures in a later chapter. Seven years earlier, on New Year's Day 1927, Paul Hicks from Leeds has unearthed a match report of a Yorkshire Junior Cup-tie between Monkbridge Sports and Leeds University YMI, apparently trumping the lot. That is not quite the research gold it appears. YMI stands for Young Men's Institute - a youth club run by the university, rather than a team from the university. That is confirmed by the treasure-house of ancient knowledge that is Harry Jepson, who could, in theory, have been at the match. He agrees that this could not have been a team of university students; but it may well be the first to have the word university in its name!

Beyond that, Sod's Law dictates that the day this book goes to the printers the phone will ring or the e-mail will chirrup and someone will tell me about a game under Northern Union rules at St Andrews in 1895, or about the Venerable Bede gathering together a few acolytes for a game of tick-and-pass with a rag-stuffed sheep's bladder on the sands of Northumbria. Until then, Peter Tate and his motley Portsmouth crew in their second-hand Castleford jerseys rank as the legitimate founding fathers. They have not exactly put up statues in their memory on the Solent or anywhere else, but they would not be out of place.

For a lasting impact, however, we have to look 300 miles to the north.

2. Ancient History:
1966 and All That

On first acquaintance, Andrew Cudbertson seems an unlikely revolutionary. Quietly-spoken and, without wanting to make him sound like Clark Kent, mild-mannered, he is, by his own admission, no firebrand orator.

Yet, when barely out of his teens, he was the man whose actions changed forever the game he loved and still loves. If student rugby league has a single founding father, it is this bespectacled, semi-retired public transport consultant, pointing out the view from the house in the North Wales village of Gorsedd, where he has lived for the last 27 years.

You look over the Dee and the Mersey, past Southport and, on a clear day, all the way to Blackpool and beyond; on a very clear day, there is a smudge on the horizon that has to be the Isle of Man.

When three student mates chatted on a train journey between Leeds and Huddersfield in 1966, they did not have even a distant vision of where their enthusiasm for the game would lead.

'There was no bigger picture in '66,' says Cudbertson. 'We just wanted to be able to play a game of rugby league.' In his case, it was a passion born in his home city of Hull. Brought up in Hornsea and Cottingham, he started secondary school in Bridlington before moving to Beverley. It was rugby union at grammar school, of course, although they were progressive enough to play the neighbouring secondary modern, which brought him up against a young Brian Hancock, later to be a Hull FC stalwart.

His father, Gale Cudbertson, was a police officer who was once given the memorable order to arrest anyone in the Threepenny Stand at the Boulevard who was using bad language. The labours of Hercules spring to mind. Cudbertson senior later retrained as a school teacher; among his pupils were David Oxley and, some years later, Niel Wood.

With the sort of serendipity that can have you declared the new Dalai Lama, Andrew was born 50 years to the day after the Northern Union - later the Rugby Football League - was formed at the George Hotel in Huddersfield. Talk about a portent if you will.

There was also something special about his approach to the sport during his boyhood, because he was one of the very few people who supported both Hull FC and Hull Kingston Rovers. In the end, he leaned a little more to the black and white, but only because his pal, with whom he went to the matches on their bikes, was a confirmed Robins fan.

In 1964, Cudbertson won a place at Leeds University, to read Chemistry, one of the wave of post-War babies who became the first in their families to go into further education in the '60s. If they have never been known for short as FIFs, then perhaps they should be.

'The demographic was changing,' he says. 'When I got to Leeds, I found that there were a lot of people there like me - people from a background where no-one had ever been to university before.'

Leeds was on its way to becoming a massive student city. Nowadays, it almost has its own student suburb in Headingley, probably the biggest and most identifiable bed-sit land in the country. It is certainly the only one with its own Super League ground, not to mention Test cricket venue.

Young Cudbertson found that it had another advantage. From Leeds City Station, you could get to all the rugby league grounds in Yorkshire and beyond. A small group of students with a mutual appetite for league, including two Cumbrians, Jack Abernethy and Bill Scott, began to pick and choose the matches they fancied.

'We were just rugby league daft in those days,' recalls Abernethy, another chemist, who went on to have a long career with British Nuclear Fuels Limited in his native West Cumbria. 'We were going to three matches a week and that's where it all came from.'

It was on the way back from a game between Huddersfield and Workington Town at Fartown that they had their Road to Damascus moment; although, given their mode of transport, it was more of a Train Through Dewsbury moment.

'We just got talking about how good it would be if we could organise a rugby league match - just between ourselves,' Cudbertson recalls. 'It turned out that we didn't have enough for a match, but we did just about have enough for a team.'

That left the question of who they were to play - and it was Cudbertson who came up with the answer. Since his arrival in Leeds, he had dabbled in refereeing and run a few lines for the likes of Fred Lindop. That had brought him into contact with the redoubtable Aubrey Casewell, the former Salford and Leeds player, who was in charge of the referees and just about everything else in the amateur game in the city. Andrew approached him for ideas on suitable opposition.

'He told me that my timing was perfect, because the Leeds League was hoping to set up an 11-a-side development division on Sundays and was arranging friendlies for clubs who might be interested in fielding a team.'

The hand-picked first opponents were General Accident, mainly composed of workers in that insurance company in Leeds, although often with a healthy sprinkling of ringers from outside.

At 11 am on March 12, 1967, a side representing a British university took to the field for the first time. They called themselves Leeds University, even though they had no permission to do so, and they were all full-time students.

Forty-five years later, Andrew Cudbertson rifles through the documents stacked in neat piles on his snooker table and I reflect on my good fortune that he has a PhD in hoarding. He has, for instance, every *Rugby Leaguer* since 1961. Where he differs from the average hoarder is that he knows where everything is. From one of the piles of paperwork, he produces with a flourish a typed foolscap sheet that carries his report of that first match. Not content with merely playing in the second row, he was by this stage an assiduous secretary as well.

The inaugural game was played on General Accident's usual pitch, on an area of Roundhay Park known as Soldiers' Field. Until the First War, it had been used for drilling local battalions; the name stuck and is still being used.

The contemporary account of the game there that day, played 13-a-side and under the relatively new four-tackle rule, strikes a tone that will be familiar to anyone who has been involved in a fledgling rugby league operation. It can be summed up as the school of 'We lost, but….'

Cudbertson wrote that:

'Despite a 15-30 defeat, this was an encouraging start, against a side who had played more than a dozen games together. Lack of match fitness was clearly demonstrated by the loss of a 12-8 half-time lead to opponents who lasted the pace better and who took full advantage of a rapidly tiring cover defence.

'Although, not surprisingly, little team-work was in evidence, there was some determined first-half play. Taking full advantage of a strong wind, Scott landed three fine goals, one of his near misses being so badly covered by the defence that, in the resulting confusion, Robinson was allowed to follow up and touch down for the first try. A second, more orthodox try was scored by hooker Dickinson, who crossed in the corner.'

It was too good to last and it is easy to imagine the rollicking General Accident gave themselves at half-time. I'll lay money that the phrase 'Come on, they're only a bunch of bloody students' figured prominently.

'After the interval, General Accident, who were well served at scrum-half and in the second row, started finding the gaps and, with the aid of three gift interception tries, gradually came out on top. With an opportunist effort, Abernethy completed the University's scoring.

'While the forwards' weak cover defence and poor combination among the backs were obvious deficiencies, there was also a noticeable lack of method at the play-the-ball. However, all were faults that practice should reduce.

'On the credit side, Clark, who played full-back at short

notice, had an excellent first-half, tackling soundly and running out well. Mitchinson, at loose forward, put in an enthusiastic performance, whilst Dickinson obtained plenty of scrum possession and worked hard in the loose.

'Team: Clark; Ross, Spink, Firth, Robinson; Cooper, Abernethy; Scott, Dickinson, Jones, Cudbertson, Shannon, Mitchinson.'

It doesn't exactly sound like a classic, but the point was that it had taken place at all. The University played other friendlies at Soldiers' Field during what remained of the 1966-7 season, including a double over West Yorkshire Foundries, who sound as though they should have been toughened in the flames, but twice had their fire doused by the students.

The feeling among those trail-blazing players was that they wanted to play on a regular basis. To do that, however, they would need money for proper kit to replace their borrowed shirts and for all the other expenses involved in running a team.

'We had called ourselves Leeds University - without permission - so the obvious answer was to make it all official and go for approved status,' Cudbertson wrote 40 years later.

'At the time, the secretary of the Union Sports Committee was a judo expert called Graham Holling and he was the guy I asked about how to form a new club. He was vaguely aware of the rugby union law at the time that any person associated with rugby league beyond school was deemed to be a professional and barred from ever taking part in the union sport. I won't repeat Graham's first words, but then he thought about the challenge and said "Why not?" He was very supportive and a great advocate for us in the debates that followed.'

Holling emerges as one of the good guys in this story.

Had he been thrown by Cudbertson's approach, university rugby league could have been postponed indefinitely. 'But if it hadn't been us, it would have been somebody else,' says the second row/secretary now. 'The time was right.' Intriguingly, Cec Thompson later recalled Jack Straw, the president of the National Union of Students and one day to occupy most of the high positions of state in Labour governments, getting involved.

It was Holling, though, who hammered out a Great British Compromise, which gave league its go-ahead without treading too heavily on the toes of suspicious union types. An agreement was forged which gave approval to the formation of a rugby league club 'provided there were no bad repercussions on the union club.'

That ambiguous clause was never invoked and neither Cudbertson nor any of his contemporaries really knew what it meant, but, as a soothing form of words, it did the job.

It could have reflected concerns over bringing the union club into conflict with the Yorkshire RU. On the other hand, they might simply have been worried about losing players - given that more and more young men with league backgrounds were making their way to universities.

The important point was that Leeds University RLFC got their £30 to cover the 1967-8 season, plus £12 for four balls. That enabled them to field two sides, one in the Saturday competition and the other on Sundays. It was a remarkable effort for such a new organisation and one that would probably not have been possible without an accidental discovery made by Abernethy, not in the chemistry lab, but in the university library.

One day, he caught a glimpse of a strangely familiar face, just visible behind a pile of books. 'I said to myself, "I'm sure that's Cec Thompson." He was a pretty distinctive figure.'

As a fanatical Workington Town supporter, Abernethy

would have had no excuse for not recognising one of the club's most celebrated recent ex-players, especially as he had met him before in equally surprising circumstances.

As a pupil at Cockermouth Grammar, he had come across Thompson shining the windows at the school, where he had the cleaning contract.

'All I could think of when I saw him at Leeds was that he must have the contract for cleaning the university too and was there to do that,' says Abernethy. 'But he wasn't; he was a student.'

He reported his sighting to his little cell of leaguies and they decided that the only way to make absolutely certain was to ask him. Sure enough, it was the former Hunslet, Workington and Great Britain second-rower. Not only that, but he was sufficiently approachable for them to ask him whether he fancied coaching their rugby league side.

'Despite being the hardest-working student I'd ever seen, he agreed,' says Cudbertson. It was a phenomenal stroke of luck and one which paved the way for the growth of student rugby league, not just in Leeds but throughout the British Isles.

The extraordinary life history of Cec Thompson is recounted elsewhere in this book. For the students of Leeds University RLFC, he was an education in himself and an inspirational personality. It was the equivalent of the university football club being coached by one of England's World Cup-winning squad of a few months previously; the sort of thing that happens informally but frequently in rugby league and rather less often in other codes.

As for what exactly a distinguished former international could impart, Thompson wrote in the club's *Handbook* for 1968-9 that he had 'mainly concentrated on demonstrating how to play the ball and interpreting the rules, since most of our players had not played RL before.'

Cec was also a mentor off the field. One weekend, Jack Abernethy mentioned to him that his two professional clubs, Hunslet and Workington Town, were playing each other in a Saturday morning kick-off at Parkside. He took his inner circle to the game in his car, blagged them into the ground with an airy 'We're with the team,' ushered them to the directors' bar and the best seats. Not only that, he took them to see the touring Australians at Headingley that afternoon, again whisking them through to the inner sanctum.

'We were penniless students,' says Abernethy. 'We probably had about half a crown apiece in our pockets, but we were on free drinks all day.'

With leadership of that calibre, it is perhaps not surprising that Leeds University achieved a respectable modicum of success in their first full season.

The Saturday team won four and drew one of their 13 games in the Leeds and District League, a competition which, in those days before regional or national amateur leagues, included heavy hitters like Lock Lane from Castleford, Heworth of York, Stanningley and Kippax.

The Sunday side, always more orientated towards the social side of the game, did rather better, winning seven and drawing one of their 14 fixtures and finishing in mid-table.

In total, it was a good effort from what was inevitably a distinctly raw set of players. That is best illustrated by the experiences of an American, Stephen Sivyer, who took up the game without ever having seen or heard of it and wrote about his first season in the *Handbook*. It all started at what most institutions call the freshers' fair, but which Leeds called the bazaar. By either name, it is the event at which university clubs - sporting or otherwise - try to get new students to sign up.

'There was a long queue at the RU stall and I noticed another "Rugby" sign further down the row of booths. I asked about rugby league and the reply was "Come along Wednesday and you'll get a game". I decided to go along for a laugh.'

That Wednesday, Sivyer made a tentative start, keeping out of the way on the wing.

'After 30 minutes of ennui, what they did in that strange grouping around the ball seemed more to my liking. I didn't come out to lope up and down the sidelines. I ended up in the second row and had continually to ask the bloke in front of me "Hey man, lemme in," which was cause for a tad of laughter.'

From that raw material, Leeds made a serviceable player, explaining the game to him before putting him onto a field.

'I looked forward to when my chance would come to drop back five yards and await the play of the ball,' he wrote. Low marks for mastery of the terminology, but full marks for enthusiasm. Sivyer played a total of 12 matches for the two sides that season and, further into his university career, made up an all-American second-row with a fellow-countryman named Higgins. It was a window into a future where student sides would cast their nets far and wide, to haul in potential rugby league players from all manner of distant waters. 'It became a joy to play,' Sivyer concluded.

The club captain that first season was a course colleague of Thompson's named Jim Shoesmith, a battle-hardened prop who had played plenty of open age rugby with Huddersfield St Joseph's. What few of his team-mates knew - because he didn't mention it - was that he was rugby league royalty. He did, however, tell Cudbertson that he was the grandson of one of the code's truly legendary players.

In fact, Shoesmith was as good as brought up by his granddad, Albert Aaron Rosenfeld, who had toured with the first Kangaroos in 1908 and had stayed on to set try-scoring records on the wing for Huddersfield. His 80 tries in the

1913-14 season is a mark that still stands to this day and he was an inaugural member of the Rugby League Hall of Fame, when it was set up to celebrate the game's centenary in 1995.

'Typically, Jim wanted it to be kept quiet from the others that he had such a famous ancestor,' Cudbertson said, recalling that first season recently. Shoesmith was clearly a tower of strength that year and became the first player to be awarded his club colours.

Other, more peripheral figures also made a telling contribution. Bev Risman, who had just returned from captaining Great Britain's Lions in Australia, had enrolled at Leeds for his MA. Obviously, the Leeds professional club, who had signed him after he had initially switched codes with Leigh, were not going to let him play in student games - just as, in a later era, Phil Clarke never played for Liverpool University, because he was already a Wigan first-teamer - but Risman was still a source of help and advice.

He took part in a question and answer session with the students that helped to raise league's profile on the campus. Much further down the track, when his playing days were over, he was to become one of the most influential figures in the growth of the game at university and college level.

Then there was Eddie Waring. The BBC commentator had become a much mocked - there were Eddie Waring Impersonation Societies at some universities - and sometimes reviled character by this stage in his career, but you will not hear a word against him from the rugby league pioneers of Leeds Uni.

At Cec Thompson's request, Waring brought his hugely popular roadshow to the university's Rupert Beckett lecture theatre. As a genuine expansionist where the code was concerned, it was very much his sort of gig. Andrew Cudbertson still has a ticket (price 2/6d) for *Rugby Round the*

LEEDS UNIVERSITY RUGBY LEAGUE CLUB

EDDIE WARING

Famous B.B.C. T.V. & Sunday Mirror
Commentator With his Show

Rugby Round the World

2 hr. Show with Colour Films & Panel of R.L, Guest Personalities
on

TUESDAY FEB. 13th at 7-0p.m.

in Rupert Beckett Lecture Theatre
LEEDS UNIVERSITY

Admission 2/6

Full house: A ticket to see Eddie

World - a two hour show with colour films and a panel of RL guest personalities - which he proffers reverentially, like some holy relic. It was a resounding success. Even at half a crown a throw, there was a full house of over 400 and 'Uncle Eddie' told Cec that he had never had such an attentive and appreciative audience.

'He would not take any remuneration for his appearance, stating that all proceeds must be devoted towards the promotion of RL in the University. Without this generosity, the club would have finished its first season in deep vermillion at the bank.'

Lurking in the background, there was always the issue of relations with rugby union, a sport which, as we will see, was more than willing to hand out life-time bans when it saw fit. That must have made prospective players, who might have preferred a foot in each camp, think seriously before playing league. Cudbertson's editorial in the *Handbook* makes it all sound distinctly cloak-and-dagger.

'To be fair, we must state that anyone of 18 years or over, who has played any form of League, is liable to life suspension from RU. However, provided students guard against indiscriminate talk, the chances of discovery by their home club are slim.

'It is pleasing to record that relations with the university RU club have in no way been strained, which suggests that this example of peaceful co-existence can be developed elsewhere in the country, particularly in other Northern universities and colleges, where I believe there is both room and demand for rugby league.'

The league club was not particularly dependent on converts from union, in any event. 'Rugby league is a sport that even at amateur level needs courage and speed of mind, as well as just the physical side,' Cudbertson wrote later. 'And so we found that talented sportsmen from whatever background (not necessarily RU) provided us with the mainstay of our teams.'

Open-age amateur rugby league was a decidedly hard school in those days; right from the start, there was something distinctive about the University's approach to it.

'Our opponents often told us how enjoyable it was playing against the University,' wrote Cudbertson. 'For once they didn't go home counting broken noses! As a rule, our games were played in a very good spirit, without any of the skulduggery that quite often featured in amateur league in those days.'

They got their reward when they were voted the 'fairest and most sporting team' in the Leeds League, the captain, Jim Shoesmith, proudly receiving their first trophy.

Of course, it is only a short step from that sort of accolade to being considered a bit of a soft touch. Unless you could stand up for yourselves at the level at which you were playing, students could easily be dismissed as effete elitists. As a hard-headed realist, Cec Thompson, knew that there was a potential problem here.

'Another notable feature was the disposition of the students' attitude towards the actual playing of RL and that of the regular club player in the Leeds League,' he wrote in that first *Handbook*.

'The students' approach seems to be a form of exercise to release inhibited reactions, whilst their opponents have a determined will to win since the game is often the focal point of their social life. Members of the committee felt as though fixtures would be better balanced if students played against students, or against opposition more of their own age and experience.'

Without necessarily realising it at the time, Thompson had spelled out the nature of next stage in the development of student rugby league.

The bigger picture, of which those three lads on the train had been blissfully unaware a few months earlier, when they merely wanted a game of the code they preferred, was about to emerge. It would not be one of clamping student teams onto existing structures, but one of setting up and running their own show.

3. Economics:
The Extraordinary Journey of Cec Thompson

Nobody in this book epitomises the breaking down of barriers quite like Theodore Cecil Thompson.

It sits admirably with the history of the game that the first black Englishman to play rugby league for Great Britain should also be a pivotal figure in another breakthrough - the one that saw a previously excluded sport come to be played throughout the country's universities and colleges. Throw in the way that Cec Thompson re-invented himself after his playing career and it is clear that we are in the presence of a remarkable individual.

Cec was born in Birtley, Co. Durham, in 1926. 'My father was a jet-black Afro-Caribbean from Trinidad, who died when my mother was pregnant with me,' he wrote in his essay on his life in *The Glory of their Times: Crossing the Colour Line in Rugby League*.

Most of his early years were spent in various orphanages

in Leeds and, as a rare mixed-race child, he was subjected to vicious verbal abuse. School was an uneven struggle and he learned little. It was not a promising start in life.

When children were evacuated from Leeds during the War, he was the only one not taken in by a family - because of his colour.

'I heard the word "nigger" for the first time and did not know what it meant. Everyone stared and pointed at me. I never saw another black face in a city of 500,000.'

Things were no better during National Service. 'I felt like a social outcast,' he recalled. 'As though I belonged more to the third world than to the Royal Navy.'

Back in civilian life, as an uneducated black man, his only prospect was of a lifetime of menial jobs and manual labour - until rugby league rescued him.

'I was a lorry driver's mate in one of the factories in Hunslet…. [they] must have been desperate, because I was chosen for the works rugby league team in a local competition. I did not want to take part in this rough game, but my pride was greater than my fear, so I played. I must have done something right because within two games I was a professional rugby player.'

Incredible though it sounds, Cec was spotted by a Hunslet scout and signed for them for the undreamed of sum of £250. Rugby league has turned many lives around, but few as suddenly and as sharply as that.

It was not quite an instant transformation. Cec started out in the 'A' team, as reserve sides were known in those days, and broke his leg during his first season. His mother died and, at one stage, he decamped to London to work as a kitchen porter, sleeping out in Hyde Park at night. By the 1949-50 season, however, he was on his way to establishing himself in the first team. The *Daily Herald* wrote after a victory over St Helens that 'Thompson impressed with his pace, speed on the ball and dogged persistence. He works his way through the game with an enthusiasm and stamina unequalled elsewhere in the Hunslet side and at the final whistle he is usually going as hard as he was at the start. He has now pretty well established himself in the second row of the pack. Hunslet has a rule that a player gets his blazer after 15 games and this was the darkie's 15th.'

Cec reproduces that article in his autobiography, *Born on the Wrong Side*, without comment on being described as 'the darkie.' He always said that he had encountered no prejudice among his team-mates; the only time he was insulted by an opponent he was given a tearful apology by no less a figure than St Helens and Great Britain's Alan Prescott. He does, however, make this observation about the world outside the changing rooms and the different forms of stigma: 'It was bad enough to be black. Now I found, if I told anyone I played rugby league, that I had acquired yet another label. How much lower down the social scale could one go than be seen as a black, uneducated rugby league player who was also an unskilled, manual labourer?'

Despite, or just possibly because of that ingrained inferiority complex, Cec now made rapid progress on the pitch. He had an influential advocate in Eddie Waring, who 'was fascinated by my exuberant style of play and did his best to get me selected for Great Britain in the first Test against New Zealand in October 1951, little more than four years after my first stumbling match for the Hunslet works team.' According to Cec's autobiography, Waring went so far as to write that: 'If Cec Thompson is not selected for the Great Britain squad, the selectors must be racists.'

He was not, as has sometimes been claimed, the first black rugby league player to represent his country. The Cumberbatch brothers, Jimmy of Broughton Rangers and Val of Barrow, played for England in the 1930s and Roy

Francis, then also with Barrow and already a Welsh international, won his GB cap against the Kiwis in 1947. Thompson was 'only' the first black Englishman to play for Great Britain when he faced New Zealand at Odsal. His side won 21-15, prompting what even he called an attack of hyperbole from the eminent Alfred Drewry in the *Yorkshire Post*, who dubbed him 'Hunslet's living bronze'.

'He reminded me for all the world of one of those old bronze figures that were once all the go for mantel decoration,' wrote Drewry. 'An athlete poised with one foot on a ball, needing only wings to be too good for this earth.' Phew. They don't write them up like that any more.

Cec also played in the second Test victory at Swinton, was one of the game's most recognisable players, but records that he remained 'terribly insecure as a person.' One source of embarrassment was the inevitable attentions of autograph hunters. He was still functionally illiterate and had to print out his name laboriously. In that image, we can feel the hunger to make up for lost time in his education that was to characterise his later life.

In 1953, he moved to Gus Risman's Workington Town, but did not play for Great Britain again. 'For all Eddie Waring's enthusiasm and my own strength and fitness, I was just not good enough for international rugby,' he wrote. 'But I like to think I scaled some pretty lofty heights in the years to come at Workington.'

That was undeniably the case, as he was a key player in Town's successes and near-successes in the 1950s, before moving on to coach Barrow. The Workington club had provided him with a window-cleaning business to supplement his playing income and it was through that work at various local schools that he glimpsed another life. He became fascinated, literally on the outside looking in, by the way a good teacher could hold the attention of a class and decided, in his quietly determined way, that this was what he was going to do.

It meant starting from basics, with English 'O' level in a class otherwise made up of young nurses at Workington College. There and at Huddersfield he built up the qualifications to study Economics at Leeds University, sitting German three times and Maths twice in the process, as he refused to be deflected by initial failures. At Leeds, he stayed on for a fourth year to take a Diploma in Education, making it seven years in all before he fulfilled his ambition to teach.

By then, he had made his crucial contribution to the birth of student rugby league, and he remained closely involved with rugby, in one form or another, for the rest of his life.

His first teaching post was at a genuinely mixed-ability comprehensive at Dinnington in South Yorkshire. There and in his next job at Chesterfield Grammar School, he was also put in charge of a rugby union side. In both roles, it is clear from his pupils' testimonials what an inspirational figure he was. At the highly traditional Chesterfield Grammar - where boys still doffed their caps to teachers - he was head of the Economics department, although his lessons seem to have ranged far and wide. 'Anyone who had a spark of ability was encouraged to make the very best of himself,' wrote one of his pupils. 'We often felt we were pushed too hard, but later we understood and appreciated the part you had played in our success.'

Much the same applied to his rugby coaching, although Cec admitted to never entirely mastering the mysteries of the union rule-book. His attempt to improve his knowledge brought him, after all the barriers he had negotiated in his life, up against one that was still intact. He enrolled on an RFU coaching course at Bisham Abbey, carefully leaving out any reference to his rugby league background.

Inspiration: Cec and Anne Thompson
with their signed match ball at
Workington Town v Swinton in 2001

'I had learned to avoid any mention of rugby league when in the company of these union buffs. I said I had been president of Leeds University Rugby and omitted the word "League." It was a shameless deception, but it worked.'

Only up to a point. 'On the last day I was asked whether I had played rugby league. I was taken aback to have such a direct question put to me on the last day of the course when I thought I was home and dry.

'.....I was the only one who was not awarded a coaching certificate. I detected a whiff of apartheid about this decision that had nothing to do with race, but everything to do with the rugby codes.

'I find it bad enough, and sad enough, that some people should dislike me because of the colour of my skin. How much worse and how much more ridiculous that I should be cold-shouldered because I had played the "wrong" sort of rugby. The apartheid system which rugby union imposes on professionals, past as well as present, should be extinct in a society that calls itself democratic.'

Cec Thompson was writing in 1995, just around the time of the first stirrings of professionalism in rugby union, but he was seeing the bigger picture, as it related both to student rugby league and to the wider world outside academia; in fact, he was uniquely well-placed to see it.

He taught at Chesterfield Grammar for 17 years, his retirement in 1991 co-inciding with the closure of the school. After that, he concentrated largely on his business in Cumbria, which had grown from a window-cleaning round into a major industrial cleaning company employing 620 people at its peak - a third strand of success, after his rugby and teaching careers, in a truly remarkable life history. That life and its achievements was celebrated in accolades which included an honorary MA from Leeds University and the freedom of the Borough of Allerdale, where he made his Cumbrian home. Student rugby league and its development remained one of his great sources of satisfaction and he continued to be an iconic figure at games and events, despite the effects of Parkinson's disease later in his life. No-one fortunate enough to meet him could fail to be impressed by him and his continuing contribution to the game that had transformed his life.

'I am absolutely astonished by the roaring success which Student RL has become,' he wrote. 'Truly, out of a tiny acorn a mighty oak has flourished.' Cecil Theodore Thompson deserves his full share of the credit for tending the fragile plant in its early years. 'I cannot deny that without me it might never have got off the ground in the way it did,' he wrote - not boasting, but merely stating a fact.

Cec died in 2011, at the age of 85. In his obituary, Professor Tony Collins, of the International Centre for Sports History at De Montfort University, put his life into context.

'His story is probably unparalleled in British sport, never mind rugby league,' he said. 'Where he came from and then ended up is almost unbelievable.'

4. Chemistry:
The Catalyst That Caused a Chain Reaction

Sometimes the chemistry is just right.

It just so happened that the nucleus of the first university rugby league club at Leeds consisted of several Chemistry students. It also happened that, for some reason lost in the acrid fug of a busy laboratory, Leeds University chemists played their counterparts from Liverpool at rugby union once a season.

Andrew Cudbertson went up to the Leeds University playing fields at Weetwood for the game, not because he was particularly interested in it as such, but because some of his mates were playing. Socialising afterwards, it emerged that several of the Liverpool side were actually rugby league players at the weekend for various north-west clubs.

Cudbertson had another of his 'wouldn't it be great if….' moments and the idea of a league match between the two universities was born. It was scheduled for March 15 1968, on the pitch almost directly across the road from what was then Naughton Park, now the Stobart Stadium, the home of Widnes - the Chemics, as they were known. The *A to Z* calls it the Leigh Recreation Ground, but it nearly failed to see the action that made it one of student rugby league's historic sites.

A couple of days before the match, Liverpool got in touch to say that they were having trouble raising a team. The easy thing for Cudbertson to have done would have been to postpone, but the club president, Cec Thompson, was having none of that. He insisted that the fixture must go ahead, with Leeds providing Liverpool with surplus players if necessary. In the event, Liverpool had a full team. It was an early lesson in what was to become one of the guiding principles of student rugby league - that the show must go on, even if circumstances look unpromising or some improvisation is needed in order to get it or keep it on the road.

It would be an exaggeration to say that this inaugural match caused a massive stir in the world of rugby league. Leeds's 45-13 win did, however, command its own little corner of the *Daily Telegraph*'s then comprehensive sports coverage. Under the heading 'University Rugby. Leeds win first 13-a-side game,' it recorded that: 'For the first time two university teams met in a Rugby League match yesterday, Leeds defeating Liverpool at Widnes.

'Leeds fielded players who assist their team in the Leeds Amateur Rugby League, but it was the first time that Liverpool had ever had a Rugby League side.

'John Priestley, a chemistry student, who comes from Huddersfield and is a prime mover in the project at Liverpool, said he hoped the team would get recognition from the University Union.

'Tries were scored for Leeds by Knowles (3), Bulless (2),

Thomas (2), Davies, Clark, Rowland and Shoesmith, while Blackburn kicked six goals. Garland, Thompson and Monk scored tries for Liverpool, Monk converting twice.'

Another article published that same day showed that it was not just a matter of turning up and playing a game of the type of rugby you preferred. In the *Lancashire Evening Post*, under the headline 'Varsity RL players to go on "trial",' Maurice Chesworth reported that: 'Thirteen mud-covered university students walked off a rugby league pitch yesterday…. and prepared for a top level interrogation.

'For the students - from Liverpool University - have been accused of "professionalism" by their Athletic Union.

'The controversy began when they formed a Rugby League team at the University, which is renowned as a Rugby Union stronghold.

'Over 18s playing League are classed as professionals, they were told by the Union.

'"Now we are being investigated and will have to report details of this game," said second year chemistry student and captain, John Priestley, from Huddersfield.

'Their opponents at the Leigh Recreation Ground, Widnes, were a team from Leeds University…. who ARE recognised by their Union.

'"We are planning to join the Merseyside Amateur Rugby League. If we are supported by the University we would receive a grant to help us," said John. "We are prepared to carry on playing regardless because everyone is so keen." Five of the Liverpool side are converts from Rugby Union. "It's just a matter of playing the game that you like best," said John.'

As rugby league has discovered down the decades, it is rarely that simple. The issue of recognition rumbled on in Liverpool, prompting this editorial, which does not fudge the issue of class, in the *Rugby Leaguer*.

'News that the proposed Liverpool University team have had their application to play League football put back for a month to allow the Athletic Committee time to look into the professional aspect of the game, strikes me as a bit peculiar, as the suggested team wish to join an Amateur League.

'I respectfully suggest the committee follow the example of Leeds University and allow the students to play the game that they themselves choose.

'It would appear that the attitude of this committee is a little outdated. In this affluent society, one does not need a hyphenated name to attend a university and if some of their students choose the League instead of playing Union the committee should not stand in their way.

'I shall be very interested in the outcome of this venture.'

The outcome was that, belatedly and grudgingly, Liverpool got their recognition and became the country's second established university club. Like Leeds, they had a significant helping hand from a well-known figure in the professional game. Mick Naughton was a senior referee from Widnes who also coached the university team. It was his links with the secretary of the Widnes Amateur League, Terry Clayton, that led to that first match being staged in the town.

With their grant, Liverpool were able to put together a diverse fixture list for the 1968-9 season. Among their opponents were St Helens Tech - another early adopter from the college sector - Hillingdon of the London League, the universities of Leeds and Bradford and amateur clubs like Culcheth and Hemsworth.

'The finest hour of the team,' said the club's end-of-season review, 'was in the defeat of International Harvesters (Bradford) with the pack conceding, on average, two stones per man.

'The club is particularly proud of its record of never

having been penalised for rough play in any game all season.

'The coaching of Mike Naughton has enabled many players to make the transition from Union to League more easily than would otherwise have been possible. The club has maintained good relations with the University Rugby Union Club and especially with the groundstaff at the University fields….

'The club considered making an application to join the South West Lancs Amateur League, but decided against it because:

a)   The standard of play is too high and new players soon get demoralised and lose interest if they are being continually heavily beaten.

b)   The turnover of students is such that the playing strength of the team could not be maintained at any level from season to season.

c)   Competitive football of our standard is best provided by inter-university fixtures.

In other words, the future lay not in backs-to-the-wall heroics against the hulking behemoths of International Harvesters - only a team called International Steamrollers could sound more heavy-duty and intimidating - but in competing against their own peers on a level playing field.

Meanwhile, across the Pennines in Bradford, wheels had been starting to turn and people were coming to the same conclusion.

The newly-formed university club was accepted as an affiliated member of the Bradford and District League, which meant that they could play friendlies and cup matches, but not league fixtures. Despite wins over Yorkshire Bus Co in their first couple of matches - you wait for years and then two come along at once - they often found themselves battling out of their weight division.

'The pack as a whole was too light,' the club's end-of-term report admitted. 'Although the second-row men were enthusiastic enough, keenness was no substitute for poundage on most occasions.'

Bradford's other problems included 'the lack of a pitch, a strip or any financial or moral encouragement from the powers-that-be. However, once the side registered some success on the field, assistance on the administrative level began to be forthcoming,' wrote their secretary, Bing Crosbie.

In theory, the club also had the help of a high-profile coach, Bradford Northern's huge signing from Welsh rugby union, Terry Price, a goal-kicker so good that he was, later in his varied career, a success in the NFL in America. However, the season's report notes rather plaintively that: 'Due to his playing commitments and the bad weather last year, Terry was only able to have one session with us, but we hope to increase on this number this year.'

The report does not ring with excessive confidence.

'The future of the club is rather in the balance as half the team from last season were final year students and… the side could be struggling. In view of this, and the fact that term times will not practically allow, we withdrew our application to join the local league, for this season anyway.' Another vote for student versus student as the main focus of activity, but before that could become a reality it needed more teams to spring up.

Salford were the first to do so as a direct result of events in the professional game. Their section in the handbook notes that: 'With the reawakening interest in rugby league in this city due to the success of the Salford senior side, several members of the university felt they would like to form a rugby league team of their own.'

The Red Devils of the late '60s were certainly glamorous enough to spark the imagination. They imported players of the calibre of David Watkins, Maurice Richards and Keith Fielding from rugby union and Friday nights at The Willows - an innovation in themselves - were a social as well as a sporting occasion.

Watkins and the Salford coach, Griff Jenkins, lent their expertise on training nights. 'Then, after a slight brush with the rugby union club's interests, we were recognised by our Students Union.'

They had a grant, a strip and 40 members - but no fixtures. The local *Manchester Evening News* solved that problem, sending their eminent rugby league writer, Jack McNamara, to meet the team and report on their problem. 'This interview led to us receiving more offers of fixtures than we could possibly hope to play.'

Their first-ever game, though, was against another university side, 'the highly polished Leeds team tearing holes in our inexperienced ranks' for a 42-6 scoreline.

At nearby Manchester, the new club had its own problems - like no shirts to play in. The Manchester and District League came to the rescue by lending them a spare set. After some humming and hawing, the league club was accepted by the university's Athletic Union, opening up the access to funding and facilities.

Manchester had some heavy defeats to well-established local amateur clubs, like Folly Lane and Langworthy. Nevertheless, they finished their first season in buoyant enough mood to plan to play both university and Manchester and District League matches the following season.

They were also the only club to supply pen pictures of their players to the first *University Rugby League Clubs Handbook,* and they give an insight into the personalities of these early participants.

I like the sounds of the hooker, Mike Massam: 'A character, whose agility on the field is nothing compared to his speed in the pub after the match. Enthusiastic on the field and a talented ball-getter, but must try to attend training more often.' One imagines that there would be one or two of them in every side; the trouble comes when there are 13.

Prop Roger Smith is 'without doubt the most ungainly runner the writer has ever seen.' There is a touch of the could-do-better about some of the other assessments. Alan Pinder, loose forward, captain and secretary, 'must try to improve his sharpness and technical knowledge of the loose forward position,' for instance.

Whatever their individual strengths and weaknesses, the students of Manchester had made a decent start. It was also at their Students Union that they hosted the most significant off-field event of the inaugural season. On March 9 1969, representatives of the five existing clubs agreed to form the University Rugby League Clubs Association.

Andrew Cudbertson, by now graduated from Leeds, was elected secretary - and he still has the minutes.

'The meeting opened with a lengthy discussion on the status of rugby league within the universities and the difficulties imposed on university RL clubs by the rugby union bye-laws on professionalism. The Bradford delegation described recent difficulties regarding their refused entry to the University Sevens and also the trouble experienced by a group of students at Leicester University who wished to form an RL club.'

Bradford had asked the Universities Athletic Union to

approach the Rugby Union, but they refused to get involved, because 'not enough time had elapsed for full consideration of the topic.'

URLCA (the first of a long series of acronyms to run the student game) voted to tackle the issue head on by writing 'directly to the Rugby Union pointing out that the particular bye-laws which outlawed participants in the rugby league game were especially unacceptable in communities such as those of universities..... that they be open to all student ordinary members, irrespective of race, colour or way of playing the ball.

'If the Rugby Union were to treat students, who had not completed their education at university and who wished to play university RL in the same way as they do RL players in the Forces, or anyone under the age of 18, then the Rugby Union itself would benefit.'

There was no doubt that this was the main issue facing the fledgling association, something that was underlined by a message of support from the secretary of the RFL, Bill Fallowfield.

'The movement was beset by problems from its inception, problems which one would think would have no place in a free democratic society,' he wrote.

'I am, of course, referring to the fact that adults who have played rugby league football have been suspended from playing rugby union in the past. I deliberately write "in the past" because I hope that the wind of change is now blowing and that it will be recognised by all that a game such as rugby league, whose patron is Her Majesty the Queen, can be played without fear of any unpleasant repercussions from any other sporting organisation.

'I sincerely hope that the University Rugby League Clubs Association goes from strength to strength.'

Fallowfield was to get what he declared to be his wish.

With five clubs established and recognised, a fixture list was drawn up for the 1969-70 University League.

The distinction of playing the first genuinely competitive inter-university match fell to Bradford and Salford and, by the time the league kicked off, there was a sixth team - from Sheffield, the first university from outside what might be regarded as traditional rugby league areas to take up the baton.

Peter Tate, formerly of Portsmouth Poly, was the founder and the survey of their first season pays tribute to his 'leadership and energy, without which the club would probably not have survived and flourished.'

The other key figure was one of the country's leading referees, Fred Lindop, who was based in Wakefield. He proved adept at coaching players whose previous exposure to rugby league had been minimal or non-existent. His message to newcomers to the code was this: 'I would recommend that you give the game a fair chance, particularly if you have only played rugby union before. Although the games are basically similar, there are many technical differences, just as there are between tennis and badminton, and this is why coaching in the early stages helps so much.'

It took a little while for that coaching to take effect, Sheffield losing their first six University League games before winning their next four. They also found the going tough in reasonably local fixtures against the likes of Kettlethorpe Hotel, Rossington Hornets and Fred Lindop's home club, Eastmoor. Nor did they have much success in the Universities 11-a-side Challenge Cup or the other new competition, the Student Sevens, although they did field a 'B' team in both those events and in a friendly against a new side at Nottingham University.

If Sheffield represented the first wave of geographic

expansion, Nottingham and Lancaster - both from well outside the mainstream - were not many months behind. More predictably, Hull were next in line, with the help and support of another great man of the game, Johnny Whiteley.

For Hull, Nottingham and Lancaster, the 11-a-side tournament provided an entry point.

It was Lancaster who made the most of it, beating the comparative veterans of Salford and losing narrowly to Leeds in the semi-finals, Leeds going on to beat Liverpool in the final at a windswept Odsal.

The Sevens gave a first outing to the Colleges of Education of Hull and Bingley, bringing closer the day when an extra initial would be needed and URLCA would become UCRLCA with the addition of a C for College. The real upstarts of the Sevens, staged at Langworthy, however, were Combined Salford Grammar Schools, including David Burke, later a professional at Rochdale Hornets and a prolific rugby league journalist. They had the temerity to beat the benchmark Leeds side in the final.

More to be expected was Leeds' success in the main competition, winning all ten of their University League matches and qualifying to meet second-placed Bradford in the final for the Eddie Waring Trophy at Headingley. The pioneering locals won 21-14 and Waring, who presented the cup, said that he had not been so excited by a match for months.

Leeds' winning line-up gives some insight into the mix of backgrounds that was a feature of student rugby league from the start. There were players from Hull, Wakefield, Wigan and Leigh, but others from Norwich, Newport, Derby and Brighton. Full-back Graham Hunter, who made a match saving tackle on Bradford's speedy centre, Harry Brown, when there was only a single point between the sides, was from Bristol.

The Bradford pen pictures go into rather more detail. Winger Gerry Bowers, for instance was 'a long-haired Leninist from St Albans and known as "Snorbins".' Then there is Rick Rawlinson, 'known as "Pretty Boy"… Due to a RU hangover he is inclined to kick when he should not.'

I think we've all met him, haven't we?

5. Geography:
Re-drawing the Rugby League Map

The map of rugby league in England had its longitude and latitude defined in 1895 when the leading Lancashire and Yorkshire clubs broke away from the Rugby Football Union over the issue of compensation for wages lost by working class players.

Those were the origins of the dreaded M62 corridor, although it was more of a Liverpool to Hull railway-line corridor in those days. Both militant expansionists and those in favour of dour consolidation in the heartlands invoke the M62 as rugby league's crucial landmark.

Of course, it isn't as simple as that. Even along the motorway, there are rugby towns and football towns. In Lancashire, a vague equation that coal mines equal rugby league used to hold good; so it did too in the Castleford-Featherstone area and well beyond M62 territory in Cumbria, but not in South Yorkshire. The intricacies of the sporting geography of the North of England needs an in-depth study of its own and even that might not make complete sense of it.

It is rugby league's proud boast that it has long since broken out of its straitjacket. After all, we have two professional clubs, one of them 30 years old, in London. We operate on a smaller scale in Gateshead, Wrexham and Neath and a further sprinkling of new semi-professional clubs, from unlikely places like Hemel Hempstead and Northampton (later replaced by Oxford), were due to come into the Rugby League in 2013.

Go down a level or two and another claim - a rather more impressive one - can be made. With the occasional exceptions of the Highlands of Scotland and the tip of Cornwall, everyone in Britain is now within striking distance of a rugby league club. This is a remarkable achievement; what is often under-appreciated is the major role that the student game has played in re-drawing the rugby league map.

The bridge-head was Sheffield, then a straight-down-the-line soccer city - in fact the original soccer city - neatly divided between Wednesday and United and with the Sheffield Eagles still not even a glint in Gary Hetherington's eye. It was not a place to which you went to further your rugby league education, unless your name was John Roberts.

At this point, I must declare an interest. John is one of my oldest and best mates; we played rugby together at school - which at our grammar school had to be union - and league for various ad hoc teams for years after. Although he was two years younger than most of us, he was incomparably the best player of the bunch. He was an organiser on the pitch, a natural reader of the game, wiry strong and a tremendous kicker of the ball. If he'd had an extra half-yard of pace - alright John, maybe a full yard - he would have fulfilled his ambition of signing for his beloved Wigan. He got as far as 'A' team trial matches under the familiar alias of AN Other. 'When you get to that level, you realise your limitations,' he says now. By way of compensation, he was a major figure in the student game; it was through him that I became aware that there was such a thing.

In 1971, John went to Sheffield University to study Materials Technology; that's okay, I don't know what it is either. 'I knew they played rugby league there. It wasn't the only factor in going there, but it was a factor.'

When he arrived at Sheffield, he was able to join a squad coached by Fred Lindop, then the country's leading referee. Naturally, there was no excuse for any side groomed by him not knowing the rules, but Roberts remembers him as a good coach in other respects - and one who knew what his team needed.

'We had players with plenty of pace and skill,' John says. 'What we didn't have was the toughness.'

The solution was to arrange a series of 'friendlies' against the hard nuts of the Wakefield and District League.

It was a rude awakening for some of the students, but the experience undoubtedly toughened them up. The result was that a city with a negligible rugby league history became the new powerhouse of the student game. Sheffield won the student version of the Challenge Cup twice and twice topped the league table, only to lose the Championship final when they fielded injury-weakened sides against Salford and Liverpool.

I am looking at a team picture from 1973. John Roberts, long-haired and heavy-bearded, is glowering on the front row. He looks like a young Charlie Manson; but, hey, this is the early 70s and so do most of his team-mates.

One exception is the clean-shaven and relatively clean-cut Lionel Hurst, scrum-half and captain, and destined to play a variety of roles in rugby league in years to come.

Lionel is one of those characters whose name crops up again and again once you start rummaging around in rugby league outside the mainstream. He has been the driving force behind the emergence of Nines as a development vehicle for the game, the man behind the Oxford Cavaliers and, perhaps a little more whimsically, the chief executive of the London Broncos in their pre-Harlequins phase. He would now be best described as rugby league's ambassador to the South-West, a diminutive blur of energy involved in all manner of initiatives in Cheltenham and Gloucester, including the University of Gloucestershire All Golds. If I had to choose someone to give me a rousing speech before I climbed out of the trenches into enemy machine-gun fire, I think Lionel would be the man. You might still get mown down, but you would feel a lot happier about it.

He will crop up again in other contexts in this narrative, but in the early 70s he was a law student at Sheffield and now thinks he must have been aware that they played rugby league there when he applied. He had already established his credentials as a rugby league enthusiast not afraid to approach the game from a different angle.

Brought up in Warrington, where his father was the club's doctor, he played league there as a schoolboy, until he was sent away as a boarder to Ellesmere College in Shropshire. There, inevitably, it was all rugby union and he shone at it, playing in the same First XV as Bill Beaumont, the future England captain and long-serving *Question of Sport* panellist.

You can take the boy out of Warrington, but you can't take Warrington out of the boy. The 14-year-old Lionel Hurst led a delegation to the headmaster - Ian David Stafford Beer, himself a former union international who sounds like a whole three-quarter line on his own - to ask whether, of all the heretical concepts, they could set up a rugby league society. This would be a better story if he had instantly had them all flogged, but Beer was not that sort of head.

'He said he had no objection, but why didn't we be really radical and make it dual-code,' Hurst recalls. 'So that's what we did.' A joint venture like that in the mutually antagonistic mid-60s was radical indeed.

When he got to Sheffield, he was collared at the freshers' fair by the familiar figure of Fred Lindop.

'He had his stall set out in a little alcove before the rugby union section, so that he could intercept you before you got any further,' Hurst says; not that he needed a lot of persuading about where his rugby future lay.

He looks back now on a successful side. 'We won a few trophies and we had a good team from a variety of backgrounds; there was John Roberts and myself at half-back and, if I remember rightly, our centres were from Eton and Harrow. Then there was John Hawley, a winger from Herne Bay who we called Cherokee.'

What he, like John, will never forget is Lindop's battle plan of hardening them up with games against Wakefield League sides.

'We played a lot of mining villages and there's no doubt about it, it was tough.'

He remembers arriving at one ground right next to a pit-head and hearing a rumbling from the bowels of the earth, followed by a metallic crash. It was the cage bringing the miners to the surface, lamps still burning in their helmets.

'Sure enough, it was them we were playing,' says Lionel with a shudder of recollection. 'In the end, I could only get a team together at the weekend by always pretending that we were playing Wakefield GPO, because we thought we'd get beaten up less by them.'

When they got the pitch and found they were actually playing another team of giants rough-hewn from the seams beneath, it could be passed off as some sort of administrative error.

Lindop had already brought Sheffield a long way. 'At my first training session in 1969, we had eight players and one of them was a 20 stone prop in Billy Bunter glasses who couldn't walk, let alone run. But he was keen and that was all I wanted,' he says.

The factor that made Lindop determined to build something from this unpromising start was the obstructive attitude he encountered from the university's head of sport, the former Welsh international rugby union prop, John Robins.

'He put every obstacle he could in our way. At training, for instance, we were allocated the area inside the 'D' at the edge of the penalty area. It was bigotry personified.'

Nor did he always get the support he would have liked from the RFL. 'I remember talking to Bill Fallowfield and he asked me what I was doing. I told him and he said "the Rugby Union won't like that." I thought what a strange thing that was to say, but then he was rugby union through and through.'

Lindop's strategy of immersing his team in grassroots league paid off handsomely.

'It was a good test for them and they didn't shirk it,' he says. The result was that they not only won student trophies, but - uniquely - carried off a cup from the outside world. That was in 1972, when they won the Wakefield and District Under-21s Cup, beating that prototypical pit village club, Sharlston, breeding ground for the Fox brothers and Carl Dooler - and a total of three Lance Todd Trophy winners at Wembley.

Fred spent 18 years coaching Sheffield and naturally

remembers outstanding players like Roberts, Hurst (whom he recalls as 'very eloquent and not a bad little scrum-half') and Hawley. Roberts, in particular, was recognisable as a kindred spirit. 'He used to belt 'em in training,' he recalls. 'I asked him what he thought he was doing and he said "I'm finding out whether they've got what it takes, Fred." Eventually, someone stood up to him, hit him back and put him on the seat of his pants. He said: "He'll do me, Fred".'

Not quite the gentlemanly ethos of student rugby league there from Roberts; must have gone to a rough school.

There was someone else, though, whose career path was to bring him back to Sheffield in latter years, with far-reaching consequences.

'Gary Hetherington played for me. He was at Doncaster Teacher Training College. They didn't have a team, so he was allowed to play for his nearest university. He was obviously a pretty fair player and we only had him for a year before he signed for Wakefield. We gave him an insight into Sheffield and he eventually came back there and set up the Eagles.'

The germ of the idea that eventually brought the city a Challenge Cup-winning team can be traced back to Hetherington's games for Sheffield University.

Appropriately, after all their ups and downs, the Eagles have been the professional club most inclined to look for talent in the student game, as well as the one playing in a stadium built for the World Student Games.

Sheffield were not the only success story from beyond the reach of rugby league's conventional geography. Unless you go back to the earliest years of the Northern Union, Lancaster is another city with little in the way of a league tradition. It could have been a staging-post between the rugby league areas of South Lancashire and the Cumbrian coast, but it never quite happened.

Not until 1970, that is. A group of students from the Manchester area had decided during the first term of the academic year that they would like to form a rugby league team. The inaugural captain, Alan Arnison, takes up the story.

'Unfortunately, Lancaster was some 30 miles away from the nearest amateur league and with the season already under way it seemed unlikely that enough fixtures would be found to justify forming a club, and so the idea was shelved and the intention was to start the team in time for the 1970-71 competition.

'However, in February we were invited to enter the URLCA 11-a-side knock-out cup competition, and within a few hours of receiving the letter we had gathered about 15 people who were willing to turn out.'

They did better than anyone can have expected, winning at Salford in the first round and beating Leeds Seconds before losing narrowly to the unbeaten Leeds first team in their semi-final. Their problem by then was who to leave out.

'Our experience here may, we hope, be of encouragement to any students thinking of starting the game in non-rugby league universities,' wrote their captain. 'We feel certain that if you ask people to play rugby league they tend to reply yes and promptly forget about it, but if you have obtained a definite fixture before they are asked the interest is much greater and the battle of raising a team three-quarters won.'

One successful convert signed up in this way was the rugby union forward, Mark Cairns, whose play in his first season of league is described thus: 'His work-rate in all the matches was exemplary and amazing considering that he has yet to reach full match fitness. His one bad point was the habit he developed of running himself into the ground and getting knocked unconscious in the last ten minutes of every match he played in.' It sounds like a brief but glorious career in the making there.

Lancaster also benefited from the coaching of an ex-pro, the former Barrow player Tommy Dawes.

Another facet of their success was an unashamed emphasis on the social side of the game. As early as 1970, they were making this proud claim: 'There are five bars on the campus and we hope that visiting teams will join us in taking advantage of them after the matches. We already have the reputation of being the best club socially in the university....'

Other significant newcomers to student competition were De La Salle, in Middleton, near Manchester, the first college of education to be welcomed into the fold. Despite also having to compete against a strong rugby union tradition, they established themselves quickly enough to win the Combined Colleges Trophy - the new cup for second tier teams - at the end of their first season. Apart from their league fixtures, they also managed 'outreach' matches against Peter Wilson's Corby Pioneers, improbably thriving in the Scots-dominated Northamptonshire town, and Bolton College.

Elsewhere, there were setbacks. Hull University and Leeds Polytechnic (forerunners of Leeds Met Carnegie, of whom much more later) contested the 1972 Challenge Cup Final, with Hull winning, but the following season neither could fulfil their fixtures. There was more stability at Huddersfield Polytechnic, another referee-coached side, with Billy Thompson at the helm.

By far the most exotic new bloom in the foliage, however, was at Loughborough Colleges.

Loughborough, then as now, had a mighty reputation as a specialist sporting forcing-house. The entire rugby league team and committee, however, came from the College of Art and Design. Like a few other developments in this saga, they came about largely as the result of a lucky accident.

Fred Lindop, as was his wont on his regular drives between his home in Wakefield and Sheffield, picked up a hitch-hiker who he described as a 'John Lennon lookalike - granny glasses, beaky nose.' That was Peter Griffin, a fine arts student at Loughborough, but also a rugby league player for a pub team, the Black Horse, in Wakefield. Naturally, this odd couple fell deep into conversation about rugby league, which led to Lindop being asked whether he would come to Loughborough to help set up a rugby league club. Not only did he do that, but despite his previous commitments with Sheffield he agreed to coach them as well.

'I had all sorts - painters, jewellers, silversmiths. It was like coaching a load of hippies.'

By 1973, UCRLCA was listing 15 members, including Manchester Polytechnic, Portsmouth and Reading, but not Nottingham, who had come and gone. Even without them, though, it was clear that rugby league's footprint extended, through the student game, to terrain where it had never been before. The time was ripe for another great leap forward, one that would take student rugby league across national frontiers.

The idea of a student international against France had been on the agenda since the inception of the first university sides in England. There is a letter in the files from October 1972, written by a M. Roques Williams of the Universite des Sciences Sociales de Toulouse and addressed to 'Monsieur le responsable de universitaires treizists anglais,' suggesting a representative fixture. Indeed, without the major expense of travelling to or from Australia and New Zealand, it was the only way of staging a student 'Test.' The issue was where and when it could be played. The Willows was available on

April 18 the following year and both sides agreed to that date, even though it was during the home team's Easter vacations.

Selection was based on two representative matches. Yorkshire beat Lancashire by a single point in a curtain-raiser before the Swinton-Whitehaven game, whilst a URLCA XIII lost to the Southern League at Eastmoor, after being refused permission to use the Sheffield University pitches. The late switch meant that some of the selected students missed the match.

In the English Universities side to face the French, six clubs were represented, with four players from Salford and three apiece from Liverpool and Sheffield, whose Roberts was named captain. He remembers that the French definition of what constituted a student for rugby league purposes was subtly different from the English interpretation. Their centre, Bernard Guilhem, was already a full international who went on to win 11 French caps, whilst the prop, Manuel Caravaca, was another who was destined to play in Tests. To be fair, England also had one professional player, in John McGuire, of Salford University and Workington Town

The French won 17-11 and the report at the time noted that 'many of the England players were short of match practice. This was apparent on the field as the French players man-for-man looked that bit faster and fitter than did the English.'

The game was played under the four-tackle rule, which was international practice at the time, and was of a standard that surprised many who were watching students play for the first time. Salford's Graham Shaw was England's man of the match from loose forward, whilst the points came from tries by another Salfordian, John Ramsdale, and Liverpool's Neil Kilshaw, plus two goals and a drop-goal from the boot of Roberts. The ubiquitous Lindop was both coach and referee, although Bradford's Ian Spurr took over the coaching duties on the night.

The teams at The Willows were:

> ENGLAND: Hawley (Sheffield); Ramsdale (Salford), McGuire (Salford), Learoyd (Leeds), Greenhalgh (Liverpool); Kilshaw (Liverpool), Roberts (Sheffield, capt); Doughty (Liverpool), Brighouse (Salford), Bartimote (Liverpool), Jones (Sheffield), Bridge (Manchester), Shaw (Salford). *Substitutes*: Hampshire (Lancaster), Meadows (Leeds).
> FRANCE: Martre; Gely, Guilhem, N'Daye, Ramel; Barthe, Cavailles; Caravaca, Cassin, Averseng, Aribaud, Sirvain, Duberge. *Substitute*: Conte.

England were only a point behind and still very much in with a chance until injury time, when the future Test forward Caravaca 'made a strong run up the middle and, after drawing three English tacklers… threw out an amazing pass over his shoulder into the grateful arms of a sprinting Ramel, who touched down under the posts.'

Given the turbulent history of Anglo-French internationals, at any level, the contemporary account in the UCRLCA handbook concludes with a rather plaintive thought.

'It is hoped that future games will be played in the same spirit as was this first historic encounter which was played in a most sporting way - a credit to two teams who gave their best.'

John Roberts played in the return game against France in Montpelier the following year, alongside Leeds's Trevor Hunt, his team-mate at school and for years to come at Leigh Miners, the top amateur side he joined having failed to make the cut at Wigan. He became a full BARLA international and a member of the first touring party to Papua New Guinea.

Hunt, who has promised to buy a copy of this book if he gets a mention, went on to become a leading commentator on BBC Radio Manchester. In France in 1974, he was struck by the apparent maturity of their students. Apart from Guilhem, they fielded five Carcassonne first-teamers. 'They were huge,' Hunt recalls. 'After the game, they were asking us things like "Where's Roger Millward." We said "Hang on, we're only a student team".'

Roberts' England and Sheffield team-mate, John Hawley - described by Fred Lindop as 'fearless in every respect' - stayed on in the Steel City, on the staff of the university, becoming deputy director of Corporate Information and Computer Services. He died in 2008 and there is now an all-weather pitch, especially suited to rugby league training, and a memorial garden outside the sports centre, both named in his honour.

Someone called Bernard Guilhem now appears to be the mayor of Saint-Nicolas Courbefy, a rural area near Limoges. If that rings a bell, it is probably because he figured in the news in 2012, when the uninhabited village of Courbefy, on his patch, was up for sale for 300,000 euros. French rugby league's do-everything man, Louis Bonnery, on the other hand, thinks he is now a dentist in Narbonne.

As for the indefatigable Fred Lindop, he maintained his commitment to student rugby league and, indeed, to any sort of rugby league that needed refereeing or coaching.

I will never forget his performance when he officiated for my club, Bolton, against Bocholt in Germany. At one stage, the Bocholt scrum-half froze like a rabbit in the headlights when he should have been feeding the ball into the tunnel.

'I'll sort this out,' says Fred. 'I speak German. Oi, Fritz, putten ze ball in ze scrum.'

After a senior career that included 22 internationals and countless major finals, he became the RFL's first controller of referees and was awarded an MBE for his tireless service to the game. He refereed in the Pennine League into his 70s and even now, at 74, he works for his son's building supplies business.

'Retire?' he says. 'And do what? Now then, can I interest you in any industrial plastics?'

6. Law:
I Fought the Refs (and The Refs Won)

If there is one area in which student rugby league has always punched well above its weight, it is the terrain patrolled by the man in the middle.

Right from Year Zero, high profile referees have taken up the whistle to take control of university and college sides. Jack Abernathy distinctly remembers one or more of Leeds University's early games against local sides being refereed by 'Sergeant-Major' Eric Clay. He certainly took charge of the return match between Leeds and Liverpool universities.

The portly Clay was at that time by far the best-known and most recognisable referee of the day, familiar to millions from his many appearances on *Grandstand*. Despite the nickname and military rank Eddie Waring attached to him, he was actually a warrant officer in the RAF during the War and later the company secretary of an engineering firm, but his static method of controlling a match suggested military authority. 'Company Secretary Eric Clay' just wouldn't have had the same ring to it. To find him refereeing your game in the Leeds and District League would have been the equivalent of turning up for a kickabout and bumping into Jack Taylor or Clive Thomas, to cite two football referees who were once household names; or being called in from your back-street cricket at the first hint of rain on the cobbles by Harold 'Dickie' Bird. It would have been a typical rugby league thing, which does not translate easily to other sports.

Amongst other things, Clay was famous for his battles of will with Alex Murphy, a player he sent off three times. The trouble was that Clay thought he should be running the game, whereas Murphy knew perfectly well that he was.

Despite that, when Murphy was awarded an OBE in 1999, he insisted on taking his old sparring partner to Buckingham Palace as one of his guests for the investiture. It was, Murphy said at the time, something called respect.

Unfortunately, we cannot check whether rugby league's most famous referee ever exercised his authority upon any other student teams, because he died in 2007. The point is that he could have done.

What we do know is that many almost as celebrated took up the whistle for university and college teams. Not only that, but there was from the beginning a tradition of combining refereeing and coaching.

We shouldn't be surprised; this is rugby league, where anyone wearing only one hat at any given time is scandalously under-dressed. Apart from Fred Lindop's portfolio of activities with Sheffield, Loughborough and, for a while, Nottingham, the Widnes referee, Mick Naughton, was involved almost from the start. Not only did he referee the first ever university fixture between Leeds and Liverpool, he sorted out the pitch and coached Liverpool for several seasons.

Then there was Billy Thompson, the natural successor to Eric Clay as the game's 'personality referee.' The after-dinner turn he does now is pure knockabout, dwelling heavily on his run-ins with Alex Murphy, but he was taken seriously enough as a referee for the Australians to bring him around the world to take charge of the first State of Origin match in 1980.

Another claim to fame was that he was the first man to send a player off at Wembley, dismissing the Leeds captain, Syd Hynes, in 1971 for his head-butt on Murphy.

Less controversially, he coached his local team at what was then Huddersfield Polytechnic - now the University of Huddersfield and one of the numerous seats of learning involved in sponsorship of the professional game.

John Holdsworth, another who in his day was England's number one referee, also did his share of coaching students, in his case at Leeds, whilst Don Bowes coached Lancashire and English Universities.

Father Geoff Hilton emerged from a rather different tradition, that of the sporting priest, once a familiar figure in the Irish landscape, much less so in England.

Apart from his parish duties at St Osmund's in Bolton, the former policeman was also a prominent crown green bowler; that's the more difficult, distinctively northern variant - pretty much a direct match for rugby league. He was a regular on *The Panel* - a handicap held daily, usually on the green at the Red Lion in Westhoughton, basically as a vehicle for some serious betting. He was equally keen on his rugby league, refereeing innumerable and student games. As I recall, he was particularly severe on any blasphemy on the pitch.

Among his many big occasions was refereeing the Varsity match. Apart from the fact that he was a good referee, that was an inspired publicity stunt, as it was when

Julia Lee got the gig. Over a decade before the NRL introduced a second referee in Australia, Niel Wood wanted to use one for the Varsity game. Not only that, but he wanted to field the identical twins, John and Bob Connolly. For maximum effect , it might have been worth using the pair of them, but not telling anyone in advance.

If anyone has refereed more student games than Geoff Hilton, it is probably either Ian McGregor or Martyn Haigh.

McGregor is a familiar face around rugby league circles and arguably the game's most prominent Scot. He is now often employed as a match commissioner and his affability is summed up by the way that he always has a bag of humbugs, Everton mints or some such to hand around. If you had done something truly inexcusable on the pitch and he reached for his pocket, you would be uncertain whether he was going for the red card or a packet of Werther's Originals. There is another side to McGregor; give him a mouthful on the pitch and he is likely to give you one back. 'I think they know I don't take any bullshit,' he says.

Originally from Rothesay on the Isle of Bute, he came to rugby league via the firm of accountants he worked for in Huddersfield.

'We did the accounts for Huddersfield Polytechnic (now University) and that was enough to get me selected. I was rugby league's only 20-stone winger, although when I played amateur I moved to hooker and then prop. I loved it.'

He first thought of becoming a referee when he got talking to Billy Thompson at a dinner and was well on the way up the ladder before he was asked if he would help out with the students. 'They had a Sevens at Salford and they were short of referees, so that was it.'

Since then, he has officiated at 'hundreds if not thousands' of student games, including finals and internationals. 'I've enjoyed every minute of it. It's different from the cynicism you can find in amateur rugby, where they sometimes just look to take out the opposition's key player. With all due respect, you're dealing with people of a certain intelligence. You tell them what you want and they get it. If they don't get it, it's because they don't want to get it - and you know you have to do something else."

Games that stand out for McGregor include the clashes in the early 90s between Cardiff Institute and Salford, when they were the two strongest teams around. Salford were coached by Shane Hansen, the Red Devils' forward and father of Wigan's Harrison Hansen, and managed by Frank Evans, the Salford matador. Impossibly whimsical though it sounds, Evans combined rugby league and bull-fighting and his sons, Matthew and Jim, both played for Salford University.

'They were tough lads - Salford lads - and they really knew what they were doing. They had some tremendous matches against the Institute.'

Even when he became a senior referee, something he believes was delayed because of his 'not looking the part' - he could have got away with refereeing in a blazer, like Eric Clay - alongside the svelte Fred Lindop, who was then in charge of referees at the RFL, McGregor continued to officiate at student games. Not all of them were an unalloyed pleasure.

'I remember one game against France at the London Skolars. It was just about under water and, if it hadn't been an international, it would never have been played. They tried to play rugby on it, but it was just impossible.'

When we met, in Ian's favourite pub - 'Here he is, the Scottish bastard' - in his adopted home-town Huddersfield, his most recent game was between Nottingham 'A' and Loughborough 'A'. It was not the biggest match that day, but, according to McGregor: 'It was excellent - two sets of good lads and two reasonable coaches. You can tell whether they're going to be reasonable by the way they react to your first decision - and they were good.' Not that he has ever worried unduly about abuse from the touchline. 'You should be in the zone, where you pretty much go deaf. You don't hear them. I've never sent many off for swearing on the pitch either; I'm probably effing and blinding at them as well.'

McGregor has always been willing to go anywhere and everywhere to referee a game of rugby league, including being flown over to France when their referees went on strike. In one match, he got around the language barrier by using the translation services of a former Salford University player, Nick Nuttall, who was playing for one of the French clubs.

'They understood me well enough by the end, but that's what I believed in as a referee - talking to players.'

On that note, he is off, because he is refereeing an evening of Nines at Featherstone.

A couple of days later, he was match commissioner for Leeds versus Wigan. It has been a varied rugby league career since he was a 20-stone winger, but the student game has provided some of the highlights.

Martyn Haigh had his own claim to fame when he was the first-ever video referee. He was the Man in the Van - or actually the Man under the Stand - for the inaugural Super League fixture between Paris St Germain and Sheffield Eagles at the Charlety Stadium in 1996. 'I was the video referee before anyone knew what a video referee was supposed to do,' he says of that experience.

As a long-serving senior touch-judge, he sometimes ran the line for his brother, the better-known Stephen Haigh. He recalls being the man who sent Jonathan Davies onto the field for his first-team debut at Widnes. Towards the end of his parallel career in the Police, he once sneaked off one quiet Saturday afternoon to run the line at another match, forgetting that it was on television and his fellow officers were watching it at the station. He claimed mistaken identity.

Martyn went out of the professional game in style; he was the man with the flag who had the impossible task of trying to keep up with Martin Offiah when he scored the try at Wembley that left Alan Tait with twisted blood. Not a bad way of bowing out, but it was a long way from being the end of his career as a match official. He was already involved in refereeing the student game and remains so to this day, following the same 'have whistle, will travel' philosophy as McGregor.

Unlike some of his contemporaries, he keeps meticulous records of every game he has refereed. There is no guesswork, therefore, over the number of student games he has controlled. 'One thousand three hundred and forty.... six,' he reports from his files, including two World Cups and countless representative games. That figure does not include the hundreds of amateur games he has refereed and still referees at the age of 68. He was in charge of my team a few weeks ago and effectively gave us the game with a decision in our favour that baffled even the beneficiaries.

'I warned that loose forward for not binding onto the scrum,' he said. 'What can you do?'

It was the sort of decision that could get you lynched in the North West Counties Division Five (now the fun-in-the-sun North West Men's League), but with which you might just get away in the student game. That, in his long experience, is the essential difference.

'I'd say I've had more pleasure out of student rugby league than any,' he says. 'It's a lot easier to do. The competitiveness is still there, but there's never any trouble with them. They're more organised and orderly.' That will come as news to some who have tried to organise student teams, especially in the early days, but there would have been no competition between universities and colleges had it not been for the help of tireless whistle blowers like Ian McGregor and Martyn Haigh.

It is, however, as McGregor points out, a symbiotic relationship. The relatively controlled environment of student sport is the ideal place for new referees to cut their teeth. That was the way it worked for a now established Super League referee like Ben Thaler and the way it is working now for the next tranche of young officials like Tim Roby and Warren Turley. 'And, if you've done a bit at senior level, you get treated with more respect,' McGregor says. If not, there's always the ultimate sanction of the Werther's Originals.

In the office where they make match appointments, they reckon that there is one distinction McGregor and Haigh have not claimed. It is held jointly by Gary Owram and Mike Rayson and it is for The Best Excuse for Missing a Match.

Owram had to give back-word because he had discovered a dead body in one of the upstairs rooms of his pub. The Carlisle-based Rayson arguably went one better than that when he was shot in the shoulder during a raid on his corner shop.

You just can't get referees you can rely on any more, although some have gone the extra yards by being flown down from the north to officiate in matches at Exeter. When the weather is bad, it can be the only way of getting them there.

7. Politics:
The Dreaming Spires and
the Curious Case of Bob Mahuta

As far back as 1973, getting rugby league into Oxford was one of the glittering prizes on the far distant horizon.

The editor, Andy Millington, writing in that season's *UCRLCA Handbook*, celebrated likely expansion into institutions like York, Durham and Essex universities and colleges in Doncaster and Bolton.

'Surely,' he wrote, 'Birmingham University could at least raise a team and "Heaven Forbid!" how about Oxford and Cambridge.'

The exclamation mark rather gives the game away. Rugby league at Oxbridge, with all the weight of tradition and conservatism balanced against it, was a spectacularly unlikely proposition. And yet, within a few short years, it had happened, because of some very special circumstances that came into play.

From several different directions, there was a convergence

of personalities that added up to a critical mass of rugby league romanticism and resolve.

From Hull, via Leeds University, came Andrew Cudbertson; from Whitehaven, to study printing at Oxford Polytechnic from 1971-3 and to launch his rugby league magazine from an improbable location, came Harry Edgar; from Corpus Christi College came Mark Newbrook; and from New Zealand came Bob Mahuta.

Newbrook was brought up at Heswall on the Wirral and came to rugby league by a typically obscure and circuitous route. His father was posted at Castleford during the War and always supported the town's club from a distance after that. Because his dad followed Cas, Mark latched onto Leeds, and in 1975 they went on an impulse to watch them play each other.

'I just remember thinking that it was a lot better than the sort of rugby I was used to seeing,' says Newbrook. 'I'd got the bug.'

That bug has accompanied him everywhere since, through stints studying at Reading, where he took his PhD in Linguistics, and teaching posts in Singapore, Hong Kong, Perth and Melbourne. First stop, however, was Oxford, where he read Classics.

'I was unaware that there was anyone else there with the remotest interest in rugby league,' he says. But here, toiling up the tracks, comes another of those Meetings on Trains that have proved so significant.

Newbrook was on his way to Swansea to see Wales play Australia in the 1975 World Cup. He was bemoaning his isolation when a couple other undergraduates, who were also going to that game, suggested that they try to stir some interest in Oxford. They were David Ambler from New College and Angela Smith of Somerville.

They placed an advert, initially to try to establish a

branch of the International Rugby League Supporters' Federation - and out of the woodwork came Messrs Cudbertson and Edgar.

Since graduating from Leeds, Andrew Cudbertson had worked in administrative roles for various regional bus companies. By 1975, he was planning routes for the Oxford and South Midlands Bus Company and living in nearby Woodstock. He and Edgar had met each other, 'but had assumed that little could be done in the way of starting up a team in the university city,' wrote Newbrook in *Cloth Caps Amidst the Dreaming Spires* - a brief history published by the City Polytechnic of Hong Kong! 'The discovery of... fellow enthusiasts brought them back into active involvement in the game.'

The university allowed them a stall at the freshers' fair before the start of the next academic year. In fact, says Newbrook, the university was supportive from the start; it was with others that they were to have their struggles. It was a high-powered line-up on the stall, as well, including as it did the secretary of the RFL, David Oxley, himself an Oxford graduate and obviously keen to see the game played at his old university, and the League's first PRO, David Howes. Maurice Oldroyd of BARLA, who was destined to be a long-term ally of varsity rugby league, was also in contact. One important signing was the future comic performer and writer, Nick Revell, an enthusiastic club member from Pontefract, then going under his birth-name of John Revell. He is remembered as a good, aggressive scrum-half.

The most significant meeting that day, however, was with Bob Mahuta, who was to be both a mentor and a cause célèbre for Oxford. Newbrook and Co saw the big Maori strolling through the freshers' fair and their eyes lit up.

Sure enough, Mahuta, who had arrived for a two-year course in Social Anthropology at Wolfson College, had a league background, although he had played rugby union as well. In fact, finding no league club in Oxford, he had joined Old Boys RU. Although he became prop, captain and coach of the league club, his name was left out of match reports - or changed - and he continued to turn out for the Old Boys. That was until he was picked for the Southern League, of which Oxford had become members, to play against English Universities and Colleges - a match that was staged in the city.

Before that, however, on November 7 1976, Oxford played their first match, at home to Peckham of the Southern League, fielding a side that was a mixture of town and gown - locals and students. Even though it was not, strictly speaking, a university team until official recognition the following year, there was a feeling, which Newbrook captures, of citadels crumbling.

'England's two senior universities had always been regarded by rugby league men as impregnable, despite various optimistic statements early in the history of the Universities League. Professional clubs had even been heard saying that their scouts tended not to pursue too seriously rugby union "targets" with Oxbridge backgrounds, believing apparently that attendance at such centres of establishment thinking would turn a man inexorably against the plebeian, "non-U" pastime of rugby league.'

The stage was set for an inaugural match that would tackle such assumptions head-on.

Or was it? In the build-up to the Peckham game, Newbrook made a startling discovery. 'The club was, for a short time, slightly dismayed to learn that there had been a rugby league match in Oxford much earlier - in 1934, in fact. While on the one hand pleased to have forerunners in introducing the code to the area, the organisers had become accustomed to regarding their forthcoming games as historic firsts and could not help but feel that these matches would suffer in significance through losing this status.'

On the face of it, the 1934 game was an extraordinary event - a match between a scratch team of Oxford undergraduates and one drawn from the foot-weary columns of one of the "hunger marches" from the north to London that punctuated the 30s. The biggest of the marches, the one that became known as the Jarrow Crusade, was in 1936, but there were marches from the depressed north-east ship-building town in 1932 and 1934 as well. That raises the possibility that the 1934 Jarrow March called at Oxford - and the game was played. The trouble is that Oxford is, by no stretch of the imagination, anywhere near the route from Jarrow to London. The closest the 1936 march, the route of which is meticulously recorded, came to Oxford was Bedford, a good 40 miles away.

True, the 1934 march could have taken a diversion to attract some fraternal support from leftist students, or a splinter group might have forked off for a quick game of league. But what connection with the code would a group of men, largely if not exclusively from Jarrow, have had? A more likely explanation is that the march in question started in the North West, which would put Oxford firmly on a logical route to the capital.

The certainty is that a match of some description did take place. We have the word of one of the participants for that. A head-master from Manchester - and originally a native of Featherstone - got in touch to say that he had played scrum-half for Oxford that day and had broken his wrist. His name was Hughes, but other details have been lost, along with his letter. In any event, he would be close to 100, if he is still alive.

Newbrook was slightly dismissive of this apparently stunning event. 'Several of the students had little idea of the rules of league and some had thought that they were to play union when they volunteered,' he wrote, 40-odd years later. 'There was no reason to regard the game as a properly staged rugby league match, despite the commendable enterprise of those involved in organising it at the time.'

That seems to down-play it a little too much. It might have been an impromptu affair, but there's a feature film lurking there in that collision between the unemployed and the undergraduates. Better than any *Chariots of Fire*, for sure.

The other 'first' rugby league match in Oxford took place on November 7 1976, at the council-owned South Park pitch, to the east of the city. The opposition was a well-established and organised Peckham side from South London, and Oxford were relatively content with an honourable 27-6 defeat.

The other result was that, almost two weeks after that game, an ominous article appeared in the *Oxford Mail* 'warning all local rugby union players against any involvement with the growing amateur rugby league movement in Oxford, on pain of a ban by the RFU.' Although it did not say so specifically, the warning was presumed to have come from the Oxfordshire Rugby Football Union.

Oxford lost a couple of matches to another Southern League club, Ealing, before recording their first victory, 17-11 over Leeds University.

Two players, Mahuta and the Welsh scrum-half, Phil Saunders, showed good enough form in those early games to be selected in the Southern League XIII to play English Universities and Colleges in March.

The Old Boys' pitch and clubhouse had been booked for the event, but nine days before it was due to take place the club's secretary told Cudbertson 'that they had been contacted by the Oxfordshire RFU and informed that that body objected strongly to the hiring of clubhouse facilities for a rugby league function. Therefore, the hiring had to be cancelled.'

Strictly speaking, the leaguies could still have played on the education authority-owned pitch, but without use of the clubhouse that was not viable. Instead, they booked a low-lying, frequently water-logged pitch at Cowley Marsh and arranged to use Cudbertson's bus company's social club, which was nearby. It was the sort of improvisation that will be familiar to anyone who has tried to establish rugby league, student or mainstream amateur, in hostile territory. The show went on, with the Old Boys and the county RFU both subsequently denying that they had tried to prevent it.

There was a preliminary game between Southern League and Universities' reserve sides, played on Corpus Christi College's ground. For the main event, there were several hundred on the touchlines at Cowley Marsh, including the 'guardian angels' Oxley and Oldroyd, who might not have agreed about much at that time, but who were united in their support for the Oxford venture.

Billy Thompson was the referee and a thoroughly entertaining game ended with the students winning 21-5. The Universities team in the match programme makes interesting reading, with an insight into the diversity of the game at that level.

Their best-known player was Loughborough's Cormac Murphy, younger brother of Mick Murphy, then of Bradford Northern, but, over his long career, one of the most-travelled players in the game, with stints in Australia and France as well as Welsh international caps. The Universities' captain was Ken Platten, a 35-year-old former docker who was reading Law at Hull. At the other end of the experience scale was scrum-half Jim Fowler, a native of Gloucestershire who had discovered the game at Lancaster, whilst one of the candidates for stand-off was Ian Greenhorn - a fine name for a relative novice - a South African studying at Bolton College of Technology.

The player whose participation caused the most widespread repercussions, however, was undoubtedly Bob Mahuta.

Born Robert Jeremiah Ormsby in Te Kuiti and brought up in the North Island mining town of Huntly, which produced, amongst others, Tawera Nikau, he changed his name by deed poll at the age of 24 to reflect his pride in his Maori heritage. He played league at primary school, union at secondary and league again for amateur clubs until his thirties. Off the field, he became head of research into Maori Studies at the University of Waikato, and it was in that capacity that he enrolled in a two-year post-graduate course at Wolfson College.

Mahuta did in Oxford what he had always done in New Zealand; he played league and union as it suited him. That was until he got a letter from the Old Boys' club telling him that he was banned, because he had played rugby league. It was widely reported at the time that he was 'banned for life,' but Mark Newbrook says that was not the case, rather that his membership of the Old Boys was cancelled and his subscription returned.

'He did not receive any communication from the county RFU or the national RFU in London, nor was he told that he was "banned for life" - an individual rugby union club would not have the authority to do such a thing,' he wrote. As for his returned subs, Mahuta donated them to the 1977 BARLA Youth Tour to Australasia.

Whatever the precise details of his exclusion, his case became a focus for league's complaints about its treatment by rugby union. The issue was taken up most energetically by the doyen of contemporary sports journalists, Frank

Keating, with a half-page feature in *The Guardian*. In some respects, Keating, who sadly passed away himself in January 2013, was an unlikely champion of league's rights, because he was at heart a union man. Many years later, he was responsible for an infamous article around the time that union went openly professional. 'Great game, rugby league,' it said in a nutshell. 'Shame it has to die.' That sentiment raised hackles, but in 1977 he knew a case of bigotry - and a bloody good story - when he saw it.

Keating was in no doubt about who had instigated the ban. The letter, he said, had been 'sent at the instigation, apparently, of the Oxford County RFU - on orders from the game's star chamber at Twickenham.' He notes that two Labour MPs were that day in Parliament to ask the Minister of Sport, Denis Howell, 'what he thinks about sportsmen being ostracised by a body that received Government aid.'

With the clear guidance of Maurice Oldroyd at his elbow, Keating broadened out the argument by bringing in other examples. There was the Silloth RU club that took down Jim Brough's England jersey off their clubhouse wall because he had subsequently played league; there was Kim Mountford, son of the league legend Cec, who was banned by Fylde because he had once played for a Blackpool Borough junior side; there was Johnny Whiteley, who was banned from coaching a schoolboy rugby union team. And then there was the case of Reading, Oxford's nearest neighbours on the student scene.

'When Reading University formed a rugby league club a couple of years ago, the university authorities readily offered them a pitch which rugby union men also used,' Keating wrote. 'When they trotted out the goalposts had been taken down - by the university rugby club, acting on orders from above.

'When in 1974 over 20,000 people turned up at the St

Helens ground at Swansea, rented from the council for Wales' first home rugby league international for years, the local rugby union club flatly refused to open any of their bars or tea-rooms – acting on orders from above.

'And on and on……'

Peter Reed, then an academic economist at Reading, is able to amplify both those last two incidents.

Originally from Featherstone but long based in the South, he 'became involved because one of my students… told me that he and his friends were being prevented from playing RL. This was because the RU club was denying them access to university facilities… The RU campaign went to absurd lengths. In the end, the RL students gained a pitch because (i) I had sufficient clout with the university administrators and (ii) the Students' Union - at a time of major student unrest - took up the matter as a "class" issue and delivered a stinging rebuke to the university RU club.'

I like the sound of that; the Reading XIII and their fellow-travellers manning the barricades.

'What do we want?'

'Rugby league!'

'When do we want it?'

'Now!'

Reed continues: 'That didn't end the matter. An eye-witness told me that the captain of all Berkshire County RU clubs had called their players together and warned them that even just talking to myself would warrant immediate expulsion. All this became quite hilarious. Shadowy individuals would turn up at games, armed with notebooks, in order to identify any RU players taking part so they could discipline them. Even when the *Reading Evening Post* staged the *Eddie Waring Show* for us, a miserable RU wretch turned up and harangued me about leading the local youth astray.

'But perhaps the most bizarre event of all… took place

when I'd moved to the Civil Aviation Authority and was chairing a meeting at Rhoose Airport... A senior official wanted to leave the proceedings early. His reason: there had been an RL international in Swansea and some local youths had taken on a group of northerners in an impromptu game in a local park. He was part of a team of RU officials seeking to identify who'd taken part in order to "discipline" them. Could anyone make up a story like this?'

That was the temper of the times and, thanks to the Bob Mahuta case, these and other instances of blatant discrimination were dragged out in the daylight for the world to see.

It was a major propaganda coup for rugby league and undoubtedly hastened the day of the so-called 'free gangway' between the codes.

As for Mahuta himself, he was left amused and bemused by the whole business. 'Sure, I was embarrassed at first, both for the Old Boys' club and myself,' he told Keating. 'But when you think about it you can only laugh and describe it as just totally ludicrous.'

Back home in New Zealand, Mahuta found himself embroiled in other controversies. He never completed his doctorate at Oxford, because the elders of the Tainui tribe called him back to lead opposition to a power station on their land. Mahuta, apart from his experience and achievements, was pre-qualified for leadership roles with the Tainui, because he had been adopted at the age of four by the Maori King. It therefore fell to him to negotiate compensation with the Government for the appropriation of Tainui land in the 19th century. That major breakthrough left the tribe wealthy, but riven with argument over what should be done with the money.

At one stage they owned the Auckland (now New Zealand) Warriors and there was much criticism of

Mahuta's stewardship and unwillingness to listen to others. His work for the Maori nation, however, was recognised by his being made a Knight Commander of the New Zealand Order of Merit - Sir Robert Mahuta.

When he died in 2001, at the age of 61, after refusing to give up cigars and ill-advisedly discharging himself from hospital, his obituary in the *New Zealand Herald* described him as 'a flawed colossus.' The then Prime Minister, Helen Clark, said: 'The bow of the canoe of Tainui has broken.' Bob Mahuta was a man who left his mark on matters on both sides of the world.

He was not the only player who gave Oxford, from the start, a distinctly cosmopolitan flavour. An American, Bruce Cooper, was one of their early stars, scoring a hat-trick on his debut against Ealing.

A longer-term impact was made by Howard Henry, from the Cook Islands, who came on as a substitute in that game and scored a try, two goals and a last-minute drop-goal from half-way to clinch a 19-5 victory. The following week he scored three tries and two goals against Stockwell. Geographically unlikely as it sounds, he and Mahuta were selected for Yorkshire Universities in the annual inter-county match. Henry was leading scorer that season and, only slightly less impressively, returned to the Cook Islands and became Foreign Minister.

Also leaving Oxford at the time were Cudbertson and Newbrook, the latter with the aim of reviving the Reading club which, despite Peter Reed's best efforts, had ultimately been strangled, if not quite at birth then in early infancy. Newbrook has a wealth of anecdotes about the period from 1978-80, when he ran the university team there virtually single-handed.

'There were several fiascos centred on unreliable players, notably a very talented winger from Papua New Guinea who was frequently absent without notice... because of cultural imperatives requiring him to entertain visitors from PNG.

'Another guy, a hooker from Shropshire who had learned the game at Hull Uni, once woke up, quite late on the morning of an away game, in a house which he didn't recognise and in bed with a sleeping woman whom he didn't recognise and whom he found decidedly unappealing. He quietly gathered his clothes and slipped out of the house into a street which he also failed to recognise... He took some time to find a bus-stop, by which stage he had missed the mini-bus.

'This guy was later in an incident where his car went on fire on the M4 near Reading, containing what was then the only copy of his just-completed PhD thesis. He plunged back in to retrieve the volume and sprang with smouldering clothing into a fortuitously adjacent pond.

'Our first captain and star prop was a sculpture student from Wigan who quarried his own stone. One huge piece he made went through a wooden floor in the London Road buildings.'

He has two particularly poignant stories, the first of which shows that the social side of student rugby league wasn't always what it was cracked up to be.

'After one match at Birmingham, they gave each of us the price of a packet of crisps, put "We are the Champions" on the jukebox and walked out. That was their idea of after-match hospitality.'

Even worse was the trip back from another away match. 'We'd lost and, even though I hadn't played, they decided it was my fault. They dragged me off the bus and all peed on me, all the while chanting "Newbrook is a wanker".'

By any standards, that is a pretty extreme example of a prophet without honour in his own land. He denies, however, that the experience dampened his enthusiasm. He still has the bug and is now a debenture-holder at Barrow.

There, he might just bump into Harry Edgar, who now spends most of his time back in his native Cumbria. He remained in Oxford until 1980, but was increasingly absorbed by his seminal magazine, *Open Rugby*.

'I remember going to training in 1976 and taking a pile of the first issue with me,' he says. We have Oxford and his experiences there at least partly to thank for the name of that influential publication. The word 'open' had a double meaning; open and expansive on the field and, unlike rugby union, open to all. The Bob Mahuta case was, Harry says, 'part of the motivation' for a magazine that always had a cause.

'For a kid from Whitehaven, which I was, it was a shock to suddenly be somewhere where even mentioning rugby league could arouse hostility.'

Edgar relocated to Leeds and produced *Open Rugby* there for over 20 years. It was then sold to League Publications - run by two men with their roots in student rugby league - and eventually changed its title to *Rugby League World*. He moved back to the West Coast of Cumbria, where for a time he was a director of Whitehaven. Now he publishes *Rugby League Journal*, an unashamed nostalgia-fest 'for fans who don't want to forget.'

Although his involvement with the Oxford club was limited after it was recognised by the university, he had played his part in its birth. All it needed by the time he returned north was a team in a slightly paler shade of blue to play against.

Above: Leeds University v West Yorkshire Foundry on Soldiers Field, Roundhay, in March 1967. This was the second student friendly, ahead of the official start

Left: Leeds University RLFC pictured at Bodington Hall in June 1968 with the Leeds ARL Sportmanship Trophy

Below: West Grange v Leeds University at Station Moor, Hunslet, in October 1967. This is the first action photograph of LURLC's official debut season, 1967-68

Above and below: Johnson Radley v Leeds University at Station Moor, Hunslet, in January 1968. Jim Shoesmith is in possession

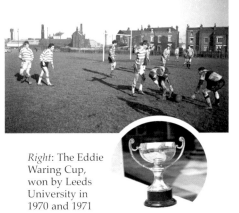

Right: The Eddie Waring Cup, won by Leeds University in 1970 and 1971

Above: Hull Uni v Nottingham Uni at Inglemire Lane, November 1970. Brian Sullivan, brother of legendary GB skipper Clive, scores one of his seven tries on the day

Above: Lancaster Uni v Leeds Uni in March 1970. An 11-a-side cup tie during Lancaster's first season

Left:
The first stirrings of rugby league in Oxford. Action from the city's South Park in the late 1970s

Right: Oxford University prepare to face Peckham in November 1976. Their yellow jerseys were on loan from from St Edwards School

Left: An Oxford University training session in January 1977, Christ Church Meadow. Note Albert Fearnley, Harry Edgar and Laurie Gant

Right: Oxford University pictured in their first official year in November 1977 at Ealing, London. Some are wearing borrowed kit!

Left: English Universities line up in March 1977 at Cowley Marsh, Oxford. They went on to beat a Southern League team, *below*

Right: The Southern League Team included the inimitable Bob Mahuta, back row - fourth from left, in their side

Left: John Revell of Lincoln College, Oxford, went on to enjoy a highly successful career in comedy

Above: Dick McConnel roars in to score a Varsity match try for Cambridge at Craven Cottage, Fulham, in April 1981.

Above: Winger Mark Oxley, son of David, on the charge for Wales in their international clash with Scotland at Knowsley Road, St Helens, in April 1988

Left: Wales lines up ahead of their Student World Cup 1989 clash with Scotland at Naughton Park, Widnes. The Welsh line up here includes coach Clive Griffiths and pioneer Dr Phil Melling

Right: The Scotland line-up, including Dr Malcolm Reid

Below: Action from the game as Wales launch an attack

Left: France v Wales in the World Cup at Naughton Park, Widnes in 1989. French winger Cyrille Pons is sent off by referee John - or is it Bob? - Connolly

Right: World Cup finalists England set to face eventual champions Australia at Central Park, Wigan, in August 1989

Left: Inches short! England prop Simon Orr goes oh, so close...

Right: The victorious Australian team lifts the Student World Cup

Above: The participating 1989 Student World Cup players gather on the pitch

Left: Wales v England in February 1990 at Cardiff's South Glamorgan Institute. Martyn Haigh is the referee

Right: Cambridge's Ady Spencer with his man of the match award after the 1994 Varsity match at London Welsh, flanked by Maurice Oldroyd and Dick McConnel

Left: Cec Thompson is reunited with fellow pioneers Jack Abernethy and Andrew Cudbertson at his Cockermouth home in June 2001

Above right: Scotland go in for a try against Ireland

Right: Four Nations winners Wales enjoy their post-match celebrations at Glyndwr University, Wrexham, in June 2012

Below: England Students in action against the Australian Institute of Sport at Kirkstall, Leeds, in December 2012

8. Classics:
Adversity, Perversity, Varsity

Oxbridge sport is a strange beast. How is one to explain up to a quarter of a million spectators standing on the banks of the Thames every year since 1829 to watch Oxford and Cambridge students row against each other?

People who have never been to either town, let alone their universities, and who know and care nothing about rowing feel obliged to support one or other of them. It isn't much of a spectacle; it is usually decided by the toss to determine the stations they occupy and only very rarely enlivened by a boat sinking or a swimming protestor. And yet it is incontrovertibly part of the English sporting summer, in a way that the universities of Manchester and Salford rowing against each other on the River Irwell - which they do - can never be.

The rugby union Varsity match still attracts wide interest, big crowds and live television coverage. The

Oxford-Cambridge cricket match at Lords still has its niche in the season.

One thing that all these contests have in common is that the Varsity game is by far the most important of the season, regardless of either team's current standing in the broader pecking order. If they play shove ha'penny or korfball at both universities, you can bet your life that the fixture that matters is Oxford versus Cambridge. Why would rugby league be any different?

England's two great university towns/cities are so automatically bracketed together that foreigners sometimes assume that they must be somewhere roughly adjacent to each other. In fact, as anyone who has arranged appointments in the two places on the same day will tell you, they are a good hundred miles apart, with no direct route between them. One suggestion for a public works project to boost the economy as the current recession began to bite was a high-speed link - either road or rail - between the two old rivals. There is no sign of that yet, so they remain warily eying each other from a distance.

If there was a rugby league team at Oxford, it followed, as the light blue skies of day follow the dark blue skies of night, that there had to be one at Cambridge. It was a symptom of another feature of their relationship, their mutual inter-dependence, that it should be a former Oxford student who made it happen.

There is a saying in Australia and New Zealand and, for all I know, in America as well that so-and-so is 'not exactly a Rhodes Scholar,' meaning that he falls short of genius level, often by some considerable margin. Rhodes Scholarships are awarded for post-graduate study at Oxford and are supposed to be for the best of the best. Bill Clinton was a Rhodes Scholar (and enthusiastic rugby union player); so were Edward de Bono, All-Black scrum-half Chris Laidlaw and, perhaps more surprisingly, Kris Kristofferson. So was Dick McConnel; in fact, we can claim him as rugby league's own Rhodes Scholar.

Although academic excellence was and is the major factor in allocating these coveted scholarships - of which New Zealand gets a mere two a year - the assessors also like to get an idea of a student's hinterland and outside interests. Thus, the future President of the United States might have mentioned his cigars, his saxophone and any other little pecadilloes, whilst Dick McConnel filled in the relevant box with the words 'rugby league'.

'I was advised not to,' he says. 'I don't think it helped.' Even that shocking admission didn't prevent his subsequent admission to study for his doctorate in Engineering. 'I just think I was lucky,' he says now. 'For one thing, there were no women to compete with in those days.'

McConnel was from Wellington and played rugby union at school. There was always an undercurrent of league in the family, however, thanks to his uncle, Arthur Menzies, a player from the Waikato who toured Britain with the Kiwis in 1926-7. At university in Christchurch, he decided to concentrate on league and was pretty much an instant success as a strong running back-rower, touring Australia with the New Zealand Students in 1969. At Oxford he reverted to another of his sporting interests, hockey.

'There was no rugby league on the horizon at Oxford at that time,' he says. In fact, he missed the start of the game there by three years. Despite both men having connections with the Waikato, he never met Bob Mahuta. Armed with his doctorate, he entered the world of work. One idea was that he would combine working on the Humber Bridge project with playing for York, but construction delays put paid to that plan. He worked on major projects in Germany and he lived for a time in Melbourne, where he once represented the state of Victoria at league and union on the same weekend.

In 1980, he was appointed as lecturer in Engineering at St John's College, Cambridge. This time he brought rugby league with him in his luggage. He contacted BARLA, who in turn put him in touch with the clubs at Oxford and Reading Universities. At Cambridge, McConnel flushed out two league-minded undergraduates, Andy St John and Paul Gamble - not to be confused with the long-serving Blackpool Borough forward of the same name. That gave them enough manpower to staff a stall at the freshers' fair and the Light Blues were on the way to having a team.

There were complications, like many of the willing players feeling they had to adopt noms-de-guerre to conceal their identities from the rugby union authorities. The favourite source of pseudonyms were the firemen in the popular children's television programme, *Trumpton*. Someone should really have smelled a rat when confronted with a pack of Pugh, Pugh, Barney McGrew, Cuthbert, Dibble and Grub. (Pugh and Pugh were twins, by the way, like the Raynes or the Beardmores.) It was the start of a proud Cambridge tradition of fake names. In the Varsity match of 1983, for instance, Simon Roberts, became the first double-blue in union and league, but played as Robert Simons. Fiendishly cunning, these Oxbridge men.

By whatever names they called themselves, though, Cambridge, within a few months of McConnel arriving, had a rugby league team - or nearly had one. For their first, unofficial, 'training' match against Oxford, they had to borrow two players. Under the circumstances, losing 43-17 to an established Oxford side containing no Trumpton firemen was a creditable effort. McConnel, a veteran by student standards, scored two tries from the second-row.

Cambridge's first official fixture was at home, on the St

John's College ground, to Reading University. Gamble, a classicist from Hull, scored their first points with a penalty, but Reading romped away to a 40-2 victory. The ex-Oxford pioneer, Mark Newbrook, was on the line, but came on for Cambridge when they ran out of substitutes, thus becoming the first man to play for both universities, despite being, by his own admission, no great shakes as a player.

McConnel initially favoured playing the first Varsity match, scheduled for March 1981, with as little fanfare as possible, because he feared that the universities - and Cambridge in particular - were not yet capable of putting on a credible show under the sceptical eye of rugby league people and a sniffy Southern media. However, Cambridge grew in confidence so rapidly that it was agreed to stage it at Craven Cottage, home of the Fulham club, whose inception the previous year had brought headlines not just nationally, but internationally. A professional rugby league club - and a successful one - was such a staggering concept that it caused a sensation. Craven Cottage was the sexiest venue that could be imagined for the first Varsity match. Unfortunately, there was some real rugby league weather around at the time and Fulham decided that their pitch would not stand up to a football match and the Varsity fixture on the same weekend. Nor surprisingly, the football took precedence and the rugby was re-arranged for six weeks later.

It was one of those matches you wish you had seen, one of those rugby league occasions you wish you had experienced. Not that the game's intermittent weather curse was entirely absent. Storms in the South and Midlands delayed the arrival of officials and guests from the North. Those guests included a number of the early Oxford stalwarts, who made up part of a 800-strong crowd in London's most atmospheric football ground. Both sides wore specially ordered new strips - dark blue and light blue, naturally, - and Oxford received the boost that their university authorities were awarding half-blues for the match; Cambridge were to follow a year later. That difference was a reflection of the Oxford club's status as by far the more established - a matter of years compared with a matter of months - but the gap was not evident from the action on the field. McConnel, playing in the backs, had his team far better organised than anyone had thought possible.

Against that, Oxford were dominant in the forwards and, in those days of contested scrums, had the lions' share of possession. They took the lead with the first points in Varsity history, from a difficult kick by Dave Symonds. The first try, however, went to the Cambridge scrum-half, Pat Mulhearn, followed by two for Oxford, from Vernon Spencer and their captain, Tim Muff. The Light Blues were struggling, but the evergreen McConnel brought them back into the game with a 35-yard run to the try-line, despite the handicap of broken ribs. They even took the lead through a try from their loose forward, playing under the name of Magrew - presumably Barney Magrew, on loan from the University of Trumpton - but Pat Wall and a storming solo from Spencer won it 16-9 for Oxford.

The teams that day were:

> OXFORD: Hallett; Canziani, Hurst, Warham, Pete; Symonds, Spencer; Gent, Lawson, Mayer, Hartliff, Healy, Muff.
> CAMBRIDGE: Raymond; Gamble, Duncan, McConnel, McGrath; Austin, Mulhern; Griffiths, Muskett, St John, Crawford, Driver, Magrew.

Mark Newbrook described it as 'a splendid match fully worthy of the breakthrough that made it possible. Those who had seen a long-cherished ambition realised on that overcast April day by the Thames could share in full in the pride and happiness. They too had played their part in bringing to pass this once most unlikely of rugby league fixtures.'

It was also the start of university rugby league's longest unbroken tradition; an annual fixture which, for better or worse, has become synonymous in many minds with the student game as a whole.

There are those elsewhere in the student and community games who believe that the Varsity match has enjoyed a disproportionate degree of attention to the level it attains. In strict, quantifiable terms, they may be right. After all, Oxford and Cambridge have never been Britain's two leading university teams. Treating them as though they are could be said to perpetuate a knee-jerk elitist approach that sits uncomfortably on rugby league's egalitarian roots.

On the other hand, we have the world as it is. The sports editors of the *Times* and the *Independent* - not to mention Sky Sports for seven years - would not be remotely interested in Salford versus Manchester, even if it was of a far higher standard. The Varsity match therefore produced - and, to some extent, continues to produce - valuable extra publicity for the code. It also provides an annual rallying point for those with a long-term commitment to student rugby league. With one or two exceptions, it usually yields a perfectly watchable match - sometimes a lot better than that.

And it has undeniably involved a diverse and fascinating cast of characters, not all of them from children's television.

Gamble, with two tries and four goals, led Cambridge to their first win in 1982 at Crystal Palace and they also won the following year at Maidstone, home to that short-lived attempt to launch a second professional team in the South, Kent Invicta.

John Risman, the son of Bev, became the first open

double-blue in 1984, as a replacement for Neil Tunnicliffe, destined in latter years to be chief executive at the Rugby League, who would have played but for a shoulder injury.

Under the coaching of Mike Penistone, who had previously put together a strong team at Trent Polytechnic in Nottingham, Cambridge dominated their rivals in the late 80s, winning three varsity games in a row. Another sign of the light blue ascendancy of those times was the emergence of their first two student internationals, Jamie Woodward and Nigel Warburton.

Originally educated at Sevenoaks, Chislehurst and Sidcup, deep in the home counties' rugby league belt, Nigel William Reginald Warburton was a hooker 'rumoured to have a brain the size of a planet,' according to the 1986 Australian tour brochure. He has lived up to that billing by becoming arguably Britain's leading popular philosopher, with Open University lectures, television programmes and books with titles like *Philosophy: The Basics* to his credit. As the Cambridge archivist, Mark Armstrong, says, hooker/philosophers are regrettably rare in today's compartmentalised world. 'Only Stevo really springs to mind,' he concludes.

For a 'where are they now?' feature in 2006, Warburton drew parallels between the two activities. 'Perceptive observers might a see a continuity in my tendency to go for the head-high tackle in debate,' he wrote.

'I loved the rhythms of the game and had always been a strong tackler and keen on fitness, so it suited me well. It took me a while to get used to running backwards when the tackle was made, though. I toured Australia with the team and the Aussie journalists fed on the idea on a hooker who was studying Aesthetics.'

In the front line of the feeding frenzy was The Australian's Warwick Hadfield (no relation).

'He has unwittingly become the most marketable member of this Cambridge side which plays in the curtain-raiser to the Rest of the World match at the Sydney Football Stadium,' he wrote of Warburton. '...because when he's not sticking his head into photography books he's sticking it into a scrum.

'At Cambridge, the fact that he's playing rugby league makes him an oddity. In Australia, the notion of a hooker with a PhD is about as laughingly probable as a politician keeping a promise.' (And this from a country that had already been captained from hooker by Dr George Peponis.)

Warburton even had a nibble at the professional game. 'The summer after I finished my PhD, I started training with what was then Fulham Rugby League Club, but realised almost instantly that I wasn't going to be signed on for a small fortune - and probably not at all - and I hung up my boots.' You could call it, were you so inclined, a philosophical reaction.

As for Woodward, Armstrong recalls him regularly riding around Cambridge on a bike with only one pedal. It actually sounds like the sort of thing one of the more marginalised philosophers might do, but Woodward is a geologist, now ensconced at Manchester University and also the resident expert for Griff Rhys Jones' series, *Rivers*. I think he is grateful to be reminded of his unorthodox cycling technique. 'It should be an Olympic event by now,' he says.

We meet at his home in Sale, along with his old school-mate, Pete Astley, who became one of the stalwarts of the Trent Polytechnic team - of whom more later - and played in the first Student World Cup. The two went to school together in Warrington, but Woodward was actually born in Leigh, which was enough to doom him to a lifetime supporting what was - just - his hometown club. He was there, as a six-year-old, when they won at Wembley in 1971 and in the rather less glamorous surroundings of Whitehaven when they won the First Division 11 years later.

A wing or centre with a burst of pace, he took up the game again when he arrived in Cambridge as a post-graduate after gaining his first degree at Aberystwyth. 'There wasn't any rugby league there, but things were really happening at Cambridge.' Just how much was happening is demonstrated by the size of the scrapbooks I cart home on the Metrolink.

Pride of place among all the documents is a letter addressed to the secretary of Cambridge University Rugby League club in 1987. It is worth quoting as an example of the sense of wonder at there actually being rugby league teams at places like Oxford and Cambridge:

'Dear Sir,

I was most interested in the scraps of news I was able to glean about your matches last season, including the Varsity match at Headingley.

I should very much like to watch your matches this season. Could you please send me information about your fixtures and where you play?

At different times in my life, I have been a supporter of Featherstone Rovers, Wakefield Trinity, Liverpool City (ever heard of them?) Halifax, Hull and Hull KR and, latterly, Fulham. Since I came to Cambridge two years ago, I've seen no RL. So you can imagine what a treat it will be.

Yours sincerely,
Sydney Fox.'

On the other hand, we have some interesting reaction from those entirely new to the game. David Hallett covered the 1987 Varsity match for the *Cambridge Evening Press* and writes like a man who has had a life-changing revelation.

'With a performance that would have brought blushes to any watching follower of Rugby Union, they played rugby that made a nonsense of the great divide between the two codes,' he wrote of Cambridge's 36-5 win.

'There were three-quarter skills that have become almost forgotten by the other lot and a level of commitment that was, dare one say it, almost professional.

'Had this been televised rather than last December's disappointing Rugby Union Varsity match, the public would have been enthralled by the skills of Jamie Woodward and Gordon Low… The pair displayed ability that transcends the great divide… Pace, handling and, above all, timing… To me, watching my first live rugby league game after a lifetime of the other code it was refreshingly different. The good players were able to display their skills without being stifled either by the bullies or simply by the less talented.

'The evidence of last night suggested that Rugby League is closer to the ideals of running and handling than its rival code, although many suggested that is not always the case in the professional game.'

Phew - mark that man down as a potential convert. Woodward has no doubt what lay behind the style of rugby that impressed Hallett so much - the coaching of Mike Penistone. 'He was just so hard-working and thorough. The coach I'd compare him to was John Monie,' he says.

That is probably no accident. Monie served his apprenticeship under Jack Gibson at Parramatta and Penistone also went to Australia to learn from the closest thing to a coaching guru the game has produced. In another ambitious move, Peter Corcoran, the ARL's national director of coaching, came to Cambridge to lecture and coach.

'He arranged his first training session for six in the morning and, when everyone turned up, he knew we were serious,' Woodward says. That sense of purpose brought Cambridge four wins out of five from 1986 onwards, with their scrum-half, Martin Woodcock, another major figure. It was Woodward and Warburton, however, who made the breakthrough to full student international status, Jamie's battle honours including the 1989 World Cup final against Australia at Central Park.

Even better than that, he got to live the dream by playing for Leigh 'A' team. 'Billy Benyon was the coach and he asked me to go down to training. I played a handful of games as an AN Other. I remember my opposite winger getting hold of me at Batley or Bramley and saying "Are you a fucking student or something?"'

He still doesn't know what gave him away.

Other notable trailblazers included John Risman, when he became the first 'open' double blue in 1984 and Ian Williams, the former Wallaby winger, who played for Oxford in 1989. The Varsity match's great cause célèbre, however, was undoubtedly Ady Spencer. The Warringtonian arrived at Cambridge in 1993 to read Natural Sciences, later switching to Chemical Engineering. His university rugby career also involved a few changes of course.

In his first year, he was man of the match in his first league Varsity match and played in another winning Cambridge side the following year. At this point, he decided he would also rather like a rugby union blue.

'I had a bit of a falling out with Bev Risman, who thought I was turning my back on rugby league, but I wanted that double blue.' (Risman headed the SRL by this stage.) Spencer got his wish in the 1994 union game. 'There was work going on at Twickenham, so the capacity was down to 50,000, but I'd never played in front of 50,000 before. I was on the bench, came on for the last 20 minutes - and then the shit hit the fan.'

The outside world vaguely noticed that Spencer had already played with distinction in the league variant and the RFL was interested in using him as a test case, by finding out what the RFU would do about it. The answer came in a letter to Spencer from Dudley Wood, telling him that he was banned for a year, not because he had played for Cambridge, but because he had professionalised himself by playing, albeit as an amateur, for the London Crusaders. Although it was frequently misreported at the time, that was what put him beyond the pale.

'If I'm honest about it, I quite enjoyed the attention and the way it showed up the hypocrisy of rugby union. I missed a tour to Zimbabwe, that would have been fun, but in the end I was only banned for ten months, because rugby union went professional. I suppose my case played a tiny part in that.'

Now living and working in Houston, Texas - 'the Yorkshire of America' - Spencer puts down the light blue success during his time there to two factors: recruitment and selection. The captain of the time, Robbie King, made sure he got his talons into any new students with rugby league experience. 'He also used to go to all the rugby union cocktail parties and picked up players who didn't quite make the first XV. There was still a bit of a fetish about recruiting union players and, if it meant leaving out people who played for you all year for the Varsity match, well, the important thing was to win.'

Ady was unbeaten in the annual big game, although his stint included the only draw between the two universities in 1994, as well as the infamous drawn 'Farsity' match of 1995, played on a partly submerged pitch at Old Deer Park. He played his fourth and last (league) Varsity match in 1996, winning another Bob Mahutu Trophy as man of the match. Watching that game with the Cambridge coach, Nick

Halafihi, was Tony Currie, coach of what was by then, for the first time, the London Broncos. He was asked to return to the club, where he started with a trial in the reserve team, alongside Currie himself, making a brief comeback at the age of 40 and hurriedly trying to mould a new gumshield in the steam from a kettle. Ah yes, the glamour of the professional game.

He made his Super League debut against Leeds, rather ill-advisedly trying to sell a dummy to George Mann - 'He absolutely smashed me' - and over the next three seasons played over 50 matches for the Richard Branson-backed Broncos, many of them off the bench as a utility player and some alongside another Cambridge man, Iain Higgins. His career ended when Gorden Tallis broke his collar-bone in the World Club Challenge at The Stoop. 'I was probably never tough enough to have a long career,' he says.

Ask him now about the overall impact of student rugby league and he pauses, not only because he is badly jet-lagged on a four-day trip home to see the Stone Roses.

'It has made a difference, but not a big difference yet. Wherever you go in the world, rugby union has an old boys' network. Rugby league has never had that and it still hasn't. In time, maybe.'

What rugby league does now have is a sprinkling of ex-Oxbridge men, prominent in all manner of fields, who know a bit about the game from playing it at university.

Exhibit A is the career of James Dingemans QC. Dingemans is a legal high-flyer, even something of a television personality in his role as senior counsel to the Hutton Inquiry. The *Daily Telegraph*, for instance, called him 'a star among the dross,' writing glowingly of 'his poise, his wit and his beautiful manners.' And where did he acquire these qualities? There is a clue as to that in his biography, where, alongside the information that his father was a rear-admiral, he is described as 'a rugby blue' - as if there was only one kind. In fact, he also played open side prop in the 1986 league Varsity match. I like to think that it was in a rugby league front row that he honed his wit, poise and manners. Ironically, given his connections, his most recent gig at the time of writing was as chairman of the independent appeal panel that ruled that London Welsh could, after all, be promoted to the Premiership.

Not all the colourful characters in the history of varsity rugby league have actually worn the light or dark blue. Take Tim Wilby, for instance, the Oxford coach for three years in the early 90s. He is described in the club's potted history as 'flamboyant,' which in my experience is usually a euphemism for something or other. In Tim's case, it was a euphemism for several things. Not that he didn't have a noteworthy and eventful playing career, incorporating as it did Leeds, Wigan, Hull (twice), Sheffield, London, the Canberra Raiders and a couple of stints in France. In fact, he scored Hull's only try in the 1980 Challenge Cup final against Hull KR - the match that emptied Humberside.

That was not his only claim to fame. When Gareth Thomas was being freely described as 'Britain's first openly gay professional rugby player,' there were those of us who asked 'What about Ian Roberts?' - although he had long left Wigan before he 'came out' in his native Australia.

I don't recall Tim Wilby ever making a formal announcement that he was gay, but it was one of those things that everybody knew. In many ways, it was one of the least controversial aspects of him.

It was Wilby who, long after his playing days were over, introduced David Lloyd - the tennis David Lloyd, not the cricket one - to Hull FC. At the time, they looked like two white knights riding over the horizon. It did not quite work out that way, but Wilby was at one stage chief executive of

Hull FC and, even more briefly, chairman of Hull City. Something about it never added up. Although Tim represented himself as independently wealthy through property deals, his only identifiable source of income seemed to be his job as caretaker of a run-down block of flats in London. It was one of those rugby league stories you couldn't make up - and at the end of it Wilby dropped out of the public view as the two clubs changed hands again.

He crops up again in the *Hull Daily Mail* cuttings files in 2010, fighting against extradition to the Czech Republic, where he was accused of smuggling amphetamines. His argument was that it was not medically feasible for him to return to an East European prison cell - where he had already spent some time - because he was HIV positive, suffering from hepatitis, life-threatening stab wounds and (perhaps not surprisingly) depression. He was, however, sighted at Headingley during the 2012 season, so he was neither dead nor rotting in a Czech jail at that stage.

Whatever else he has done with his life, Wilby was a firm believer in spreading the game of rugby league, both geographically and socially. Hence the Oxford connection. He brought a professional gloss to the operation and his side were strong favourites to win his first Varsity match in 1990. It was a match that produced a major surprise and some extraordinary coverage.

'Oxford seemed to have all the advantages. Their team has a rugby league nucleus, including players brought up on the sport here - and in one case, in Papua New Guinea. Cambridge were all union men, bar one,' wrote Peter Higgs in the *Mail on Sunday*. 'Oxford have a professional coach… Their rivals were prepared by a college lecturer who used to play university hockey.' Oxford had also had by far the better season, finishing fourth in their division, with Cambridge struggling in tenth. The Light Blues turned them over 20-15 and a mass-circulation paper like the *Mail on Sunday* devoted the best part of a page to going into paroxysms about it.

'These young men will go on be the captains of industry and the leaders of communities,' Higgs quotes the associate director of the SRL, Malcolm Reid, as saying.

'Most will return to union when their university days are over,' Higgs writes, 'but with a new respect for a sport no longer linked to the back streets of Dewsbury.'

How the players felt about being described in the headline as 'The Young Toffs' is not recorded, but the value of the publicity to the profile of Oxbridge rugby league was incalculable. In a sense, though, Oxford were victims of their own pre-match publicity, with Wilby admitting afterwards that they had been 'a bit complacent.' Not so the following two Dark Blue years, with Oxford also reaching the Premiership final in 1992. In 1991, eternal student John Hobart became the first man to play, for Oxford, in six consecutive Varsity matches. As if that is not enough, he is also the son-in-law of the Wigan (and Oxford United) owner, Ian Lenagan.

The Wilby years formed a buffer between the outstanding Cambridge sides of the late-80s and their seven-year unbeaten run in the 90s. Since then the pendulum has swung, with Oxford winning nine of the last 13. There have been solid reasons for this. Oxford's authorities have traditionally had a more liberal attitude to the arcane business of awarding Blues - full, half, discretionary and combinations of them - which has made recruitment easier.

Oxford has also awarded rugby league scholarships, something that would have seemed inconceivable to the pioneers of 30-odd years earlier. Johnnie Gorrie and Johnnie Prescott , who came to the university on that apparently unlikely basis, played in the Varsity matches of 2006 and 2007.

Going back in 2012, after a couple of years' absence, I was struck by how the event had shrunk. For one thing, national newspapers are no longer particularly interested; the novelty has worn off. Sky have dropped it and, after rattling around at The Stoop, it is back in the more appropriately scaled surroundings of Richmond. In 2013, it was due to move again, to the handsomely appointed but even cosier setting of the Honorable Artillery Company's ground in central London.

Even Dick McConnel missed it one year, when he was unavoidably on the other side of the world, leaving Maurice Oldroyd as the only devotee with a 100 per cent record. The scale of Oxford's victory - a record 48-0 - has McConnel worried. 'We can keep turning up every year and getting beaten, or we can do something about it,' he tells me afterwards.

That something has to include a bigger incentive - through Blues and the rest - to play a demanding game.

In the meantime, the Varsity match remains one of the social events of the season; a chance for those who created and continued the tradition to touch base. If it did nothing else but that, it would be worth its place on the calendar and its night in the spotlight.

9. Media Studies: Read All About It

One thing that student rugby league has always understood instinctively is the importance of media exposure. Right from the first organised, or sometimes disorganised games, university and college teams have been willing and able to trade on their novelty value to win precious column inches. From the late 60s onwards, the *Rugby Leaguer* carried regular student news. Student newspapers, always eager for usable copy, were a shop-window in which the early pioneers could grab the attention of potential players and announce: 'Hey, we're here.'

Occasionally there has been an oil-strike, like the *Guardian*'s coverage of the Bob Mahuta case, the *Independent*'s World Cup sponsorship or the *Times*'s front page picture of the 1995 'Farsity Match.' But student rugby league has never had more exhaustive coverage than it got for seven years from Ray French and Gerald Webster.

French is, quite simply, a rugby institution. A dual-code international, he has, apart from the occasional moment of madness from the union authorities, been able to pull off the tricky dance-step of keeping a foot in both camps. Some people mistrust that particular brand of footwork, but although league is his core activity, it is all rugby to Ray. Unlike some of us - guilty m'lud - he doesn't have an ounce of bigotry in him.

He is the author of a series of influential books, a Radio Merseyside commentator and, for almost 30 years, BBC television's man at the microphone, with his trademark 'Why, oh why…..?' voicing the bafflement of generations of viewers.

This media career ran in tandem for years with him teaching English (and both codes of rugby) at Cowley School. I have been fortunate enough to tour with him on a number of occasions. Many an aimless slumber under the palm trees has been enlivened by Ray's cry of 'Bollocks to it,' followed by a heavily-annotated copy of *Tom Jones* or *The Canterbury Tales* flying across the swimming pool.

Had he been born a few years later, he would almost certainly have been involved in the launch of rugby league at Leeds University. When he arrived in 1958, however, the rugby world was a different place and he was already embarked upon a union career that was to bring him England caps. Rugby league and a university education did not sit together comfortably at this stage.

Ray went to Leeds because it took its rugby union seriously. It was also, to some extent, friendly towards the other code, even though the idea of it actually being played there was still several years away. In his most recent book, *Ray French... and Rugby*, he describes the atmosphere.

'Large numbers of the students and some of the staff used to watch Leeds RL at Headingley, while others who hailed from Wigan, Wakefield, Warrington and elsewhere were the first to grab the newspapers in the university library on a Monday morning to read about their favourite team.'

I once met an elderly gent who was an undergraduate at Leeds around this time and recalled going to Headingley to see Leeds play Warrington. It had been raining heavily, so the pitch was little more than rolled mud. Straight from the deep kick-off, Brian Bevan caught the ball in the corner and set off on a typical weaving run, beating a series of tacklers to score in the diagonally opposite corner. Or did he? Because of the state of the pitch, you could clearly see his footprints and his route was... dead straight. My informant swears this is true. What I don't know is whether he was studying Geometry or Wizardry.

Wilf Rosenberg, Leeds's former South African RU winger, who could do some magical things himself, was at the university studying Dentistry. Gerry Round of Wakefield Trinity was in the Engineering department. It was not quite hostile territory the way Ray remembers it.

There could still be some ridiculous situations. Round, for instance, was invited, despite his rugby league background, to play for the Anti-Assassins - a sort of northern equivalent of the Barbarians, assembled for festival-type matches. He was so impressive that a scout from Leigh asked him whether he was interested in turning professional. Round muttered something non-commital about needing to concentrate on his exams and made his escape.

There could be a more sinister aspect. French, by then a rugby league player with St Helens, had been due to complete his teaching qualification at Loughborough. Before he could embark on the course, however, he was told that he would have to attend lectures on Saturday mornings, unlike rugby union players, who were cheerfully given special dispensation. Leeds University rescued the situation by inviting him to remain there for his diploma and he went on to have a distinguished career at Cowley School, teaching English and coaching both codes of rugby.

In his latter years there, he combined teaching with writing for Eddie Shah's *Today* newspaper, a publication whose influence has lasted rather longer than it did. When both those avenues came to an end, he found himself, by his standards, with time on his hands. He filled it by spending the next seven years of Wednesday afternoons watching and reporting on student games for the *Rugby Leaguer*. It was not piecemeal coverage either, but the full treatment, with pictures from Webster, a Francophile, bon viveur and all-purpose rugby league enthusiast.

'I enjoyed it as much as anything I ever did,' he says now. 'We went up and down the country, from Exeter to Scotland. Everywhere we went, they gave us a marvellous welcome and we saw some terrific games.

'I remember driving back from one game in Wales and both of us saying that it was one of the best matches we had ever seen - between two Welsh colleges.'

French maintains, however, that much of the importance of the games was off the pitch. 'People developed a taste and a respect for rugby league and took that with them into business, industry or the professions, where they would be the decision-makers on the future.'

Apart from that, the student game has been responsible for kick-starting a number of high-profile media careers. Tim Butcher is a classic example of someone whose future direction in life was mapped out by his experience of student rugby league.

He was not new to the game when he went to Lancaster University, having played for Wakefield Juniors and

Eastmoor. 'I was vaguely aware that there was rugby league there, but I wasn't planning to play. I think I thought it was too unfashionable and I was going to try to get in the soccer team,' he recalls. 'The year before I got there in 1976, the rugby league side lost every match - but they were just a much better set of lads. It was great, I loved it from the first match. I'd found a level where I could star.'

With Butcher at loose forward, Lancaster had some good seasons, losing a Championship final to Salford and winning a UAU final (for universities only) at Blackpool.

Like many successful clubs, Lancaster had an imaginative approach to recruitment. 'We used to go recruiting in the weights room, looking for muscley lads.' Sometimes they had American accents, because Lancaster had an exchange programme with the States. That was how they found Andy Findlay, who adapted well enough to play for England Students. He was more fortunate than another American, who was taken home for Christmas by one of his English team-mates and still bears the scars from being glassed in a pub in Normanton. That team-mate was Dave Machen, who was a good enough player to create considerable interest at professional clubs - I was asked to have a look at him for Blackpool Borough - and went on to play for the first team at Barrow.

As for Butcher, he was good enough to play for England Students, including two trips to France, one of which lives on in infamy. The 1978 international in Toulouse was conventional enough; England turned up, looked with trepidation at the size and maturity of Bernard Guilhem and company, got soundly beaten and went home. The visit two years later was a slightly different proposition. The team was billeted at the youth hostel in Aix-en-Provence, where relations with a large group of Germans were not good, even by historic standards. In between the drinking and fighting, the Liverpool winger, John Parsons, somehow got covered from head to toe in boot polish. The following morning, their coaches, Don Bowes and Ron Barnes, said 'That's it. That's enough. The tour's over' and decamped to Corsica on holiday. The squad decided to carry on without them, as there was still a match scheduled to be played at Cavaillon, which degenerated into a series of running battles.

'It was the only time in my career that I was punched by a touch-judge,' Tim says. 'A fight went towards his line and he just took a pop at me.' Among the other trouble-makers on that trip was Niel Wood, who is still blamed by Butcher for missing a series of kicks at goal that could have won the international at Aix.

After his degree in Politics and History, Butcher stayed on to take his teaching qualification at nearby St Martin's College. 'After that, I moved to London to play in a band,' he says, revealing a whole new side to himself. He played guitar in The Snorkels - a group who sound not so much underground as under water. 'We played a bit of funk, a bit of soul.' Sadly, The Snorkels never quite surfaced and eventually split up because of artistic differences. He was the manager of a betting shop, served a couple of years in the London Fire Brigade and set off overland to Australia on a motorbike with his wife-to-be. They got as far as India, before coming home with the intention moving back to the North. Tim reappeared on the rugby league radar when he became development officer for the code in Sheffield. He was there for eight years and, at its height, had over 100 schools playing the game. Over 25 years later, many of them still do.

Fate, though, had something else in mind for Tim Butcher. In one of those random long-shots that can ruin your life, he found himself, when he moved back to Wakefield, living right next door to one Martyn Sadler. It was Lennon meeting McCartney at the church fête, Bader encountering Meinhof for the first time. At the Station pub in Crigglestone, they began to put the rugby league world to rights, particularly its media coverage. 'We just thought we could do better than what was out there at the time,' Butcher says. In 1990, along with another citizen of Wakefield, Mike Rylance, they founded *League Express*.

Sadler had been a Wakefield Trinity supporter from an early age but, thanks to going to the wrong schools, never actually got the opportunity to play the game. Nor was he involved in it during his time as a student at Sheffield Polytechnic. When he became a Business lecturer there, however, that all changed. Along with one of his students, who came from Widnes, he decided to set up a rugby league club. They found a healthy uptake, much of it from players who didn't feel at home in the union camp. Sadler remembers a Yorkshire Under-19s flanker who couldn't get the sniff of a game, for the simple reason that the captain played that position. 'He came to us and was an outstanding player. A lot of the rugby union club were arseholes - all initiation ceremonies and rituals designed to humiliate people. We got a lot of lads coming to us because they wanted to play rugby without being exhibitionists.'

Mick McGowan, whose work with the Colts at Bradford Northern involved mentoring a young Ellery Hanley, came on board as coach and Sadler eventually left the students to get on with it. He had, though, discovered that administration was his forte. He became chairman of UCARLA (the Universities and Colleges Amateur Rugby League Association), taking over from Don Metcalf of Wakefield College, who sounds like a hard act to follow.

Martyn has a good story about Metcalf, a former Trinity player then well into his forties, who was on the touchline watching his side getting roughed-up by the opposition's hooker. He brought off one of his forwards, confiscated his boots, went on and sorted out the problem.

Martyn Sadler never did anything like that, but he does have one notable victory to his credit from his days in student rugby league. He had become involved in another set of initials - BPSA, the British Polytechnics Sports Association - and, as he was trying to put together a representative side, noticed that a lot of the better players were dropping out. It turned out that they were union players, who were being threatened with lifetime bans if they played league. Sadler contacted the BPSA, arguing that they should not be funding sports clubs which were not open to all.

The union clubs backed down and the principle of a free gangway was established at college level - a small but significant victory in the on-going battle against bigotry.

Sadler was England's manager for the first Student World Cup, in New Zealand in 1986. 'We found that the definition of what constituted a student differed widely,' he says.

For instance, the New Zealanders had the full international and former Wigan player, Howie Tamati, at hooker. 'He just nutted our guy at the first scrum and knocked him unconscious, which wasn't what we were expecting. We only managed to beat Papua New Guinea.'

Sadler stayed on as manager for the 1989 tournament, but his thoughts were already turning elsewhere. When Tim Butcher moved in next door, he recognised his name - not from his lead guitar work with The Snorkels, but from a case that had come before a UCARLA committee several years earlier. The hearing was to decide whether Butcher still qualified to play for Lancaster, even after moving to St Martin's College.

'When he moved in next door, I was very relieved that we had said yes,' Sadler says.

The two have gone on to form an axis that has dominated rugby league publishing for the best part of a quarter of a century. They are the tip of an iceberg of people who might have drifted into student rugby league in the first place, but who found their direction through it.

'It's hard to quantify,' says Sadler, 'but there must be hundreds, even thousands of people out there who first got involved as students.' Butcher calls it 'attracting people who would one day become the movers and shakers... and it's happened.' On the family dynasty front, all three of his sons have played as students, the eldest for mighty Leeds Met. 'That showed me how much it has changed,' he says. 'When I was at Lancaster, we would give literally anybody a game. Now at Leeds Met, they have about 100 turning up for trials. They choose the best and the rest are told to bugger off.'

There will always be casualties. What, for instance, of John Parsons, who we last encountered covered in boot polish in the South of France? Along with some team-mates at Liverpool, he published a best-selling series of study guides, later selling the company for millions. Another triumph for student rugby league.

We also have the student game to thank for a generation of writers and broadcasters who have undermined the glib contention that journalists have never played the game and therefore can never fully understand it.

My witness for the defence is the *Guardian*'s Andy Wilson. Born and brought up in leafy Macclesfield, his cultural roots were at leaky Watersheddings, because he inherited the enthusiasm for his father's hometown club, Oldham, and for the game in general. The only rugby league he had played was for a side which his schoolteacher dad, Ian Wilson, had got together at Kings Macclesfield - needless to say, a staunch union establishment. 'In theory, I could have gone to Woolston or somewhere, but realistically it wasn't going to happen,' he says. 'It was too big a gap to bridge.'

His chance came when he went to Leeds University in 1990 to read Economics (later switching to Politics). He went to the rugby league trial and was straight into the first team for the opening game of the season at the University of Northumbria and stayed in the side for his three years. 'It's the proudest I've been of anything I've done.'

Wilson had some memorable times in his three seasons and reluctantly agreed to recall them in one of Chorlton's trendier bars. There was the run to the play-offs, which saw Leeds travel to UWIC. Rob Ackerman was well into the veteran stage by this time, but, on a bad day, Andy still has a vague tingling in his shoulder from tackling him. He made friends for life, some with rugby league backgrounds, some not. He lined up with some good players, like Phil Hassan, who had a decent professional career, and Nigel 'Nudge' Borowski, who drew the short straw and finished up at Chorley. 'Not only was he a superb rugby league player,' Wilson remembers, 'he was the champion of the social side of things.'

He also got some good coaching at Leeds, most notably from the characterful combination of Peter Jarvis and Roy Dickinson, who used to arrange for the team to have their pre-match meal of beans on toast at Bramley - once served by Sonny Whakarau, Wilson recalls. Jarvis used to stand on the touchline in a pair of much-mocked golf shoes. In one match, he went on to check on the state of an injured member of the opposition and accidentally spiked him to the ground.

Once, on the way back from a sevens tournament, the Leeds bus broke down on the M62. One player was detailed to run to the nearest phone, but, in his absence, they got the bus running and completely forgot about him, until he turned up, understandably disgruntled and dishevelled, at breakfast the following morning. Ah, happy days.

It gives some sort of reading of the impact that the student game can make on young hooligans like this that, almost 20 years on, just about all Andy's old team-mates maintain an interest or involvement in rugby league.

'I suppose that's the main benefit; that and the great time we had.' There's just one thing that still rankles. 'We beat Leeds Met the year before I was there, lost to them for the three years I was there and beat them the year after I left.' It can't all be due to the way he played second-row and hooker, although he modestly suggests that it might have been, but I dread to think what Sky could prove with a stat like that. Actually, the evidence of his contemporaries is that he was a good, sound player, well worth his place in the side. But, compared to others in the same city, there was already an ideological split opening up. 'To me, it was the social side that really mattered,' says Wilson. 'That was more important than winning and losing - and that's the way it should be. Leeds Met took it too seriously.'

Despite that hint of Gentlemen versus Players, Andy took the game seriously enough to become one of its leading writers, cutting his teeth on *League Express* whilst still at university and graduating to the *Guardian*, where his job now, to his chagrin, revolves more around his second-favourite sport, cricket, than rugby league. In cricket journalism, he has observed, it is hard work to be taken seriously without Test caps. It isn't as bad in rugby league, but there is probably still a consensus that it helps to have played at some level.

Young men like Andy, who have played as students and come into the media thereafter are a valuable resource for the game. We agree over a pint that nothing gives you a better appreciation of what professionals go through than having had a try yourself. As I always tell him, from my own experience, it helps no end to have been a bad 'un, especially an educated bad 'un.

In theory, there could be a steady stream of similarly qualified young journalists emerging every year from the University of Huddersfield's Sports Journalism course. In a different twist, the university is the Huddersfield Giants' shirt sponsor, just as the University of Chester is for Warrington.

10. Australasian Studies:
Meanwhile in the Southern Hemisphere

I write at a time when a British university side is preparing to play in a professional league for the first time. The University of Gloucester All Golds - I wonder how often they will be referred to by their full title - represent a bold experiment. Typically, the Australians were there first, although only by a narrow margin of 93 years.

It was a case of seizing an opportunity. 'The promotion of the University club by the NSWRL was seen as a direct attack on the traditional home of rugby union - Sydney University,' say Ian Collis and Alan Whiticker in *The History of Rugby League Clubs*. Union had lost ground when it suspended competition during the First World War and the NSWRL pounced. In early 1920, the *Rugby League News* reported that:

'...a strong league club had been formed at the University because the men believed that it was the better game of Rugby. The old cry that boys leaving the Great Public [state] Schools, if they had played League football would not be able to do so at the University would now be a thing of the past. A special meeting of league supporters was held and decided to enter three teams, all members to play as strict amateurs.'

That did not convince the Amateur Sporting Federation of New South Wales, whose president, one James Taylor, questioned whether the students could retain their amateur status when playing against professionals. Horrie Miller, the secretary of the NSWRL, pointed out that amateur league players were free to compete in athletics, rowing, swimming and boxing. '...if you attempt to stop them... the aid of the law will be sought and you know that you have not a legal leg to stand on.'

The senior University side was to compete against the well-established district sides - Norths, Souths, Easts, Wests and the rest.

In their first match, they were soundly beaten 36-12 at North Sydney Oval. They won just one match in their first season, against Annandale, the only side to finish below them. That was despite the coaching expertise of famous former players Arthur Hennessy, Paddy McCue and Alex Burdon. That last name was a resonant one, because it was Burdon's broken arm - and the Union's refusal to compensate him - that was the catalyst for the birth of the code in Australia 12 years earlier.

The Sydney students fared better when they played Queensland University in the first-ever inter-varsity match anywhere in the world during that same 1920 season, winning 26-16 in front of a 60,000 crowd before the NSW-England match at the Sydney Cricket Ground.

University had a lot more defeats than victories, but they came good in 1926, when they reached the final - no grand finals in those days - against the mighty South Sydney, losing by a respectable 11-5.

The club had its first Kangaroo tourist in 1933, but that embarkation ended in tragedy. Wing or centre Ray Morris was taken off the ship with an ear infection at Malta and died in hospital there. Because he never got to Britain, he is not listed as a Kangaroo - and University never had another selected. They were in a downward spiral. In their last four seasons, they finished last each time and won just two games. Among their results in 1937 were a 63-0 thrashing by South Sydney, and one by 65-5 to St George. Their final game was against Canterbury and, in the third grade match, they fielded some of the veterans from their early seasons, effectively forfeiting the game. They were standing down voluntarily, having come to the conclusion that they could not compete against the mature, professional players of the other clubs.

It was not the end for Sydney University. They started playing again in 1962 and, along with the University of New South Wales, they were founder members three years later of the new Second Division competition, later known as the Metropolitan Cup. The students were once more playing against professionals; Lewis Jones, for instance, was captain-coach of Wentworthville, so they were not exactly encountering bad players, although they did get four representatives into the Second Division side that played New Zealand Under-23s in 1967.

Sydney University performed well in that division, reaching a grand final, and in 1970, along with Wentworthville, they were invited to play in the pre-season tournament with the senior clubs. They took some heavy beatings, which, according to Collis and Whiticker, 'proved conclusively that the students - lighter, younger and more inexperienced than their opponents - could not compete with the professional district clubs.' It's the old story, although told with an Australian accent.

Oddly, in view of New Zealand's sporting geography, the standard-bearers in that country coalesced at the University of Otago in Dunedin, well down towards the southern end of the South Island and with not much more rugby league heritage than Exeter or Penzance.

From 1954 until 1967, that was the only centre of further education regularly playing the game, although as far back as 1956 they played a one-off fixture against Canterbury University. For the most part, though, it was a lone furrow they were ploughing, although not always an obscure one. In the 1950s, Otago University players like Trevor Agnew, Peter Dalton and Rex Billington came close to selection for the Kiwis. In 1969, a PE student, Trevor Patrick, went one better when he represented New Zealand in the first Test against the touring Australians. He won a second cap against Great Britain the following year.

By that time, the code had spread within New Zealand, to include the universities of Auckland, Victoria (Wellington) and Canterbury, who were all playing in their local competitions. Canterbury had come out of hibernation after a 12-year snooze and had a player, Greg Gass, in the South Island team that played Australia. Auckland, then as now New Zealand's strongest division, saw its university competing on equal terms with the leading local sides, including one memorably narrow defeat by Mt Albert at Carlaw Park. Otago, under the coaching of the former Halifax player, Enoka McDonald, remained strong in their local league.

It was all encouraging enough for the newly-formed New Zealand University League Council to select a representative team for a first-ever tour of Australia - the one Dick McConnel went on. There they found a code that was also on the rise at what Australians call the tertiary level. Sydney's third university, Macquarie, started to play in 1968.

By the time the first University Cup competition kicked off, there were nine teams on the starting line, including two each from Sydney University, NSW University and Macquarie. One of the Macquarie teams, Balaclava, finished top of the table at the end of the regular season, but were beaten in the grand final by Sydney University Blues.

John Pollard, the secretary of the Sydney University club and vice-president of the University Cup, argued in the organisation's first annual report that the value of these developments was clear.

'The NSWRL realised that the university clubs had to be encouraged, for two reasons; firstly, because it was prestigious and good promotion to have professional men playing and associated with rugby league; and secondly, because universities and teachers' colleges produced the school teachers of the future who would determine whether rugby league would be the sport played by school children of future generations.'

It was a similar rationale to that which had taken root in Britain; that student rugby league was storing up credit for the code in generations to come. One thing they could not envisage in Britain was anyone doing what Trevor Patrick had done, by graduating straight from a university side to a full national team.

In the *University Rugby League Clubs Handbook* for 1970, the review of developments down under concludes: 'Whilst the likelihood of any British universities player representing his country at RL, even for the amateur international team, must be very remote in the immediate future, it is worth remembering that several notable figures in English RL have graduated in their youth from our Northern universities. Names that spring to mind are Bernard Ganley, Bev Risman,

Ray French, the late Gerry Round, Len Clark of Hull KR, John Walsh of... St Helens, and Terry Kirchin who is currently starting a further three years at York University.' One part of that prophesy was disproved when John Roberts won his BARLA caps, albeit after his student days were over.

As for the great and the good listed above, we shall see that more than one of them was destined to play a major role in the future of student rugby league.

With an eye on that future and its international dimension, the review concludes with this wish: 'Perhaps we can hope that the remarkable progress made in the last few years in all the RL playing countries will eventually lead to a Student World Cup!'

When the student pioneers stuck an exclamation mark on the end of something, it tended to denote an aspiration that might have seemed fanciful at the time, but was destined to come to fruition.

11. Celtic Studies:
Beyond the Fringe

When Wales won the Student Four Nations at Wrexham in 2012, their coach, Clive Griffiths, dedicated the victory, sealed by a memorable 20-18 win over England, to an expert from Wigan on Ernest Hemingway's life and work in Cuba.

Dr Phil Melling had died of cancer at the age of 64 the previous November, but he was not forgotten at the moment of triumph. 'It was the players who took it on board,' says Griffiths. 'But it was only right and fitting. Most of all he was a great friend, but he's also the man who revived rugby league in Wales.'

The 13-a-side game has had a chequered history in the Principality, to say the least. For all the depth of its passion for rugby union, there has always been a minority view that they made the wrong decision back in 1895. After all, the economic and social considerations that led to the birth of the Northern Union - particularly the need of working-class players not to be financially disadvantaged - applied equally strongly in South Wales. By the English rule of thumb that coal mines equal rugby league, it should have been fertile ground. The factors against it were geography, with a 200 mile gap between them and the North of England, and the willingness of the RFU to turn a pragmatic blind eye to the Welsh playing fast and free with the draconian regulations on amateurism. Long before Welsh players were going north to play league, West Countrymen were going north to play union in the Valleys - and not for love alone.

Having kept the Welsh on board at the time of the Big Split, the union authorities were determined to keep them there. What they could not prevent was the steady drain of players to Lancashire and Yorkshire, where they could be paid openly and, if successful, could go a long way towards setting themselves up for life. Phil Melling himself wrote one of the finest books on a member of this diaspora, *Man of Amman: The Life of Dai Davies*, about the Broughton Rangers, Warrington, Huddersfield and Keighley scrum-half of the 1920s and 30s. He also wrote perceptively about his boyhood hero, Billy Boston, notably in his essay in *The Glory of their Times: Crossing the Colour Line in Rugby League*.

Skimming the cream of their talent was one thing, however, planting the game in their own backyard quite another. There were several attempts to change that, the first of them before the First World War, when a series of South Wales clubs failed to take root. There was also an amateur league and a Glamorgan and Monmouthshire team in the County Championship between 1927-31, and a short-lived Cardiff club in the early 50s. Throughout the rugby league-playing career of Boston, to name the main victim, there was not even a Welsh international side, although there were plenty of Welshman who played for Great Britain. The Wales side was revived for the World Cup in 1975, but when Phil

Melling arrived at the University College Swansea, as it was then, four years later there was no organised rugby league being played in the country at any level, apart from the occasional, bussed-in Wales squad.

As described earlier, our paths had already crossed at Keele, Phil a lecturer in America Literature when neither of us knew of the other's league allegiances; perhaps I would have got better marks if we had. Born in Wigan in 1947, he had been educated at the universities of Manchester and Indiana. It was at Swansea, though, that he found the cause - or rather the range of causes - that defined the rest of his life. There he became the world's great authority on Hemingway's years in Cuba and from there that he ran an educational charity in Guatemala. He was a man of global vision, but, for our purposes in this book, he was the man who kept the rugby league flame alight in Wales.

Not content with tackling the complexities of Latin American politics, he took on another rigid and repressive regime - the one decreeing there would be no rugby league in Wales. He decided to set up a team at Swansea and he never kidded himself that it was going to be easy.

'I remember being told I would get no further in my career at Swansea if I carried on with rugby league,' he said. 'I was taken aside and told that senior people in professional and administrative positions in the college were saying I should stop straightaway. It may have been a bluff, but it was meant as a warning.' Despite that whispered intimidation, Melling persuaded enough students to have a go to raise a team, which was an immediate success in the Southern Group of the UAU (Universities Athletic Union). In the three seasons from 1979, they won that competition once and were beaten finalists twice. They also won the Southern Universities Trophy twice, beating Oxford and Loughborough in the finals. They were a little torch burning in the darkness and they were joined by another, at the Glamorgan Institute in Cardiff.

In 1987, Melling made a significant phone call to Clive Griffiths, the former Swansea RU, St Helens and Salford full-back, to ask him whether he fancied coaching a Welsh Student side in a World Cup two years later.

Griffiths had switched to rugby league in 1979, after winning his one Welsh cap against England. He had enjoyed a successful, if not downright sensational career in the North and had developed a strong gut-feeling for the game that outlasted his playing career.

'I asked him how many teams he had and he said "Oh, two or three". "How many players?" He told me about 23 or 24. I told him I didn't think that would put the fear of God into Australia and New Zealand.'

Despite his reservations, Griffiths took the job which Melling, as chairman of the Welsh Rugby League, was offering him, and Wales performed well in the World Cup in 1989 and have been in every international tournament since, winning the Student Four Nations in 2004, 2009 and 2012.

Equally important, the game has put down sturdy roots in a number of institutions. There have also been a couple of other developments with the potential to be significant.

North Wales Crusaders - who are the new club launched from what was left of the Celtic Crusaders, as originally launched in South Wales - are now effectively the tenants of Glyndwr University, who own what used to be Wrexham's Racecourse Ground. The Crusaders share a coach - Clive Griffiths, naturally - with the Welsh Students and the overlap between them is considerable. In the south of the principality, Wigan have opened a rugby academy, which they hope will enable them to tap into the cream of Welsh talent.

More conventionally, there are leagues in both North and

South Wales, and even the odd one - like the Montgomeryshire Marauders - in Mid Wales. There are a total of seven universities and colleges playing the game, including far-flung outposts like Bangor and Aberystwyth. The Valleys are a far cry from the rugby league wilderness that confronted Phil Melling when he arrived at Swansea.

If anything, Scotland has an even more chequered - maybe we should call it tartan? - rugby league history than Wales, although it has never had a professional club and any moves in that direction are now strictly on the back-burner. It is, though, a country of which it can truthfully be said that there would be no rugby league at all were it not for an initiative at student level.

At about the same time as Phil Melling was making his phone call to Clive Griffiths, David Oxley was contacting Dr Malcolm Reid, a lecturer at Aberdeen University, to ask whether he thought he could put a Scotland team together for the 1989 World Cup. Reid's name was known because, as a former rugby league player, he had ruffled the feathers of the union authorities by coaching the Scottish Students RU side. The row over his eligibility to do that had been extensively covered in the press, notably by the *Guardian*. He was, in any event, disillusioned with the union code and keenly interested in an approach from the game he had played for Barrow, Widnes and Blackpool. 'They thought I had horns growing out of my head,' he says of the SRU's attitude. He told Oxley and Martyn Sadler that he was up for it.

'I had enemies in the union camp, but the students were always on my side,' he wrote in his preface to Gavin Willacy's history, *Rugby League Bravehearts*. 'So it was no surprise to me that most of my first XV at Aberdeen took up league. I preached team unity, cohesion and hard work and the lads responded. The first year we had two or three

Sunday sessions, teaching them the basics, like the play-the-ball - an introduction to the sport. Soon we were going on pre-season trips to France, having training camps and playing amateur clubs in Cumbria.

'The progress the lads made was amazing. They'd return to their union clubs and be bursting through tackles, creaming people and confident with the ball in hand. The clubs would ask: "What the bloody hell's happened to you?"... Their union team-mates saw what league could do for your game and wanted to play too.'

The Scots' first match was at Lancaster University, coached by Reid's brother, and they continued their learning process against BARLA sides in Cumbria. Reid, now employed by the RFL, would be out and about all over Scotland, looking for potential converts. 'I'd go to union clubs and talk about this strange sport of rugby league that they'd probably seen on television... I was trying to get them to understand that league was good for them, that they would benefit from it. I wanted to change that cloth cap image; these were the future world leaders, the teachers the doctors, the solicitors. If I could get them to realise what a bloody good game league is, when the name rugby league came up, they'd say: "That's okay, that is" and want to get involved, as sponsors, administrators or whatever.'

That 'whatever' category includes a member of the House of Lords. Dominic Hubbard, aka the Liberal peer, Lord Addington, was part of Reid's Aberdeen and Scotland teams, qualifying via his Scottish mother. He wasn't quite the poshest person ever to play student rugby league, but he was close. That distinction falls to the Queen's grandson, Peter Phillips, who played whilst at Exeter University. They once had the best ever excuse for postponing a game, when the entire team was at Windsor Castle for his 21st. In 2012, he presented the Challenge Cup at Wembley.

Lords, lairds or whatever, the Scottishness of the squad was always a priority, although Irishmen Mike Kerr and Paul Gowdy played by virtue of attending Scottish universities. More statistically significant was the number of first- and second-generation Scots roped in from England.

Kevin Rudd, who was next-but-one as guiding light for the game in Scotland, says that you need a 40/60 split in one direction or the other, between natives and imports, for the chemistry to work. 'Go beyond that and the balance isn't right,' he says. A squad in which half are learning about rugby league and the other half are learning about being Scots is 'an exciting mix.' Reid had introduced the visible trappings of Scottish identity. The squad was always immaculately turned-out, a sponsorship deal with a kiltmaker enabling them to be kitted-out in full Highland dress. That process continued under his successor, Bev Risman's younger brother, John. Willacy describes the players as being 'bewitched by the intoxicating, partisan experience of representing Scotland.' Risman, who had a long professional career himself, put it this way: 'The lads got wrapped up in it all. We had the bagpipes and all that and it created such an impression that those lads were hooked.'

Graeme Thompson was Edinburgh born-and-bred, a Scottish and British Students international, who combined the roles of Scots development officer and coach to the student team. He increased the Scots content of the side, before moving on to the London Broncos and the RFL. He was replaced by Rudd, a hooker who had played for Reid in the Midlands, and was by now at Edinburgh University.

I had always assumed that Kevin Rudd, with what sounded to me like a very light accent, was a Scot who had spent a lot of time living outside the country. If he has any Scots in his voice, though, it is there by osmosis, because he comes from Garforth in West Yorkshire. He put extra emphasis on the issue of cultural immersion.

'You have to offer people something different,' he says. 'Our players had an experience they couldn't have had any other way.' Rudd's own experiences include beating England twice in 1996 - the second time in the World Cup. He was also player-coach of the Forth-Clyde Nomads, the first amateur club in Scotland and a direct off-shoot of the student game, although it required him making a 300-mile round trip.

That highlights what he regards as one of the students' major achievements north of the border. It is no exaggeration to say, as he does, that they 'created and founded the Scottish Rugby League.' The other thing in which he takes pride is 'an infectious pioneering spirit that has spread to other fledgling international federations that have since taken up the game.' In Rudd's time at the helm, the kilted and besporraned Scots went to Russia, France, Italy, Germany and the Netherlands. Without claiming any monopoly on long-distance development work, Rudd recognises a strong Scots flavour in what the RL Student Pioneers do now. Rudd is well placed to make the comparison and the connection; after his time as an adopted Scot he became the development officer for the European Federation.

Scotland have never won an international competition - there will probably never be the depth for them to achieve that - but since 1987 they have always been there, competing colourfully against nations with far greater resources. It wouldn't be a party without the Scots there.

Scotland Students have been a conduit through which talented administrators like Thompson and Rudd - who now lives in Kingston-upon-Thames but still has a faint brogue to my ears - became immersed in the game. Not that it has always been a comfortable experience. Living and working in Dunbar, Rudd found that anti-league bias could be as fierce as ever. 'In a small, parochial town like that, there was still a huge stigma. When it starts to affect you at work, it starts to bring that home to you.' Where and when has rugby league ever been the easy option?

The same can be said of those whose contribution has been purely as players. Among the notables who have come through the Scottish Students route is Nick Mardon. A real all-rounder, he represented Scottish Schoolboys at basketball, football and cricket, as well as rugby union. Whilst studying Economics and Maths at Edinburgh, he found out about rugby league and went on to captain Scotland Students and play for them in the 1992 World Cup. He later signed for the London Broncos, where an injury-affected career as a Super League full-back included playing in the famous victory over the Canberra Raiders at The Stoop.

Others for whom the Scottish Students proved a springboard to the professional game have included the well-travelled Iain Higgins and Sheffield Eagles' long-serving prop, Jack Howieson - the latter a Scot from Hemel Hempstead. Also memorable was Billy Gamba, a second-rower of Italian descent from Dundee University, who was man of the match in the 1992 World Cup win over England.

Perhaps the man with the most remarkable career since pulling on a Scotland Students shirt is Mike Rush. A scrum-half at Edge Hill College in Ormskirk, he qualified through Scots grand-parents and also played for the full Scotland side in the Emerging Nations World Cup in 1995. When his student days were over, he worked on the youth development programme at St Helens, where he was so highly regarded that, when they needed an interim coach following the sacking of Royce Simmons in 2012, it was to him (and Keiron Cunningham) that they turned.

Okay, there's no Dave Valentine or George Fairbairn in

that line-up. The little flame that was lit for the 1989 World Cup still burns, however. In 2012, Edinburgh Napier played four times in Nines tournaments with three other Scottish Unis. Rugby players come through other universities, in Scotland and beyond, as well as the much-travelled Scottish Students side and take that experience with them into a further involvement with rugby league or back into rugby union. The Scottish Conference League, which spans Aberdeen and Moray in the north to Ayrshire in the south, would not exist were it not for the students. As Kevin Rudd says: 'It's all been worthwhile for that alone.'

For the student who best illustrates the fairytale possibilities of an unexpected involvement with the game, however, we must look to Ireland and a life transformed by dipping a hesitant toe into rugby league. Brian Carney was born in Cork, although 18 months of his early childhood were spent in Kent. Back in Ireland, his first sporting enthusiasms were for the Gaelic sports - hurling and particularly Gaelic football.

'I still love it, not just for the game itself, but for the part it plays in the life of the country. Every village has a team.'

When the young Carney was sent away to boarding school, he first came into contact with rugby union, where his explosive pace was every bit as big an asset. At University College Dublin, where he enrolled to read Business and Legal Administration, he found himself gravitating towards the Lansdowne club. 'I wasn't even that keen on rugby union, but everyone told me to go down there, so I went,' he recalls.

It was there that he came onto the radar of Brian Corrigan, who since 1989 had been running the Dublin Blues league club. Corrigan had a bad case of the rugby league bug since he acquired the habit of getting the ferry from Dublin to Liverpool at the weekend to see the best match. Anyone who has travelled on those weekend ferries will not need telling that there are hundreds and thousands of Liverpool and Manchester United supporters who regularly make that crossing; rugby league converts are rather rarer fish.

Corrigan was a long-term rugby league agitator and fifth-columnist in Dublin from his teens onward. He even wrote to Bill Fallowfield, when he was secretary of the RFL, urging him to 'get something going' in Ireland. The Warrington referee, Charlie Appleton, was even sent to meet Corrigan whilst he was in Dublin, 'but I don't think he was too impressed with this 15 or 16-year-old lad.'

Undaunted, he maintained his contacts with Irish-descended heavy hitters in the British game, like Tom Keaveney at BARLA and Tom O'Donovan, who worked on development and expansion for both the RFL and BARLA. Corrigan was the obvious man to pull together an Irish squad for the Student World Cup in 1989, by which time he also had the Dublin Blues up and running. There was no shortage of amateur sides willing to cross the Irish Sea to play them, but plenty of the usual barriers that had to be cleared. 'We had a lot of problems with the availability of pitches and that sort of malarkey,' he says. 'You'd get the Union people phoning up schools and saying "You do know, don't you, that if you have this game on your ground, you won't be insured?" There was a lot of that sort of nonsense.'

Sometimes the Blues couldn't get a rugby pitch at all and were forced to use a Gaelic football ground. I can vouch for the fact that it was a good deal bigger than its rugby equivalent and not exactly ideal for 40-something prop forwards who had survived a long night on the ferry from Holyhead. At least we didn't have to face Brian Carney.

Corrigan was always on the look-out for players, from union or Gaelic backgrounds, who had the potential to adapt to league. When he saw Carney, his eyes almost popped out of his head. 'He was in my ear all the time, telling me I was made for rugby league,' Carney remembers. 'He kept on at me to have a game for the Dublin Blues and eventually I agreed.' The way Brian Corrigan remembers it, 'he was cycling past our training session on his bike and we roped him in. He just took to it straight away.'

Apart from his obvious pace, he had a kamikaze streak in him that made him special. When Corrigan says that he 'had no respect for his own body,' he means it as a compliment.

Carney's instincts might have been sound, but his actual knowledge of rugby league at that time was not extensive, limited as it was to half-watching the occasional game on television. His playing debut was against a pub team 'from somewhere in Yorkshire, who had obviously been out all night painting the town red.' It was not difficult for a bright-eyed young winger with pace to burn to shine in that company.

He was fast-tracked into the Ireland Students squad for the Four Nations in Glasgow, where I got my first glimpse of him. Like a first sighting of Martin Offiah a few years earlier, it was one of those moments that makes you stop and say: 'Hello, what have we got here?' It's easy to be wrong about the potential of young players, because some of the most obviously talented for some reason or other never make it. When you see a winger with blazing pace, though, who can catch a ball and has a real appetite for the game, then you know that there is something to work with.

Despite being surrounded by players who knew much more about rugby league than he did, Carney was named as player of the tournament.

More significantly, a video of his performances made its way - via the Irish development officer, Nigel Johnson, and his north-east counterpart, Mick Hogan - to Shane Richardson, the chief executive of the newly-formed

Gateshead Thunder. Carney, his degree course over, had been planning to travel around Australia with a few mates. It was Richardson's job to persuade him that he was better off hooking up with a bunch of Aussies on Tyneside.

The approach was not particularly subtle. The Thunder flew him over, put him in a flash hotel and took him out to the floating nightclub on the Tyne. 'And then they're wanting to pay me to play rugby. I'm thinking to myself: "How good is this?"'

Other clubs were showing interest, but the key selling point for Gateshead was that, if he went there, he would be among a group of players as new to the area and the culture as he would be. 'I thought that would help me to settle in and it did,' he says.

It was the start of a grand little career. He was part of the mass exodus to Hull, signed for Wigan and went on to play for the Newcastle Knights, before a spell in Irish rugby union and a last lap with Warrington.

He also played 14 times for Great Britain and Ireland. Not Great Britain, you understand. Great Britain AND Ireland - and, honourably, he never even pretended to sing the national anthem. He is now the rising star of Sky Sports' rugby league team, every bit as lively and articulate as a man whose name rhymes with 'blarney' should be.

And he owes it all to student rugby league. There might have been an alternative entry point, but Super League clubs do not do a lot of scouting at matches between the Dublin Blues and pub teams from Yorkshire. Not surprisingly, he has strong views on the significance of the student game.

'Important and getting more important,' he says. 'You can't afford to ignore it. Look, I'm still new to the game and its history and culture, but I know that, at one time, if you were looking for rugby league players, you just shouted down the nearest coal-mine. That's all gone now; the equivalent of the coal-mines now are the universities,' he says. It's an intriguing idea - that today's pit-heads are to be found on campuses.

He agrees with the contention of the Sheffield coach, Mark Aston, that the closest thing to professional athletes are young men who are taking sport seriously at universities and colleges. That doesn't mean that players like Brian Carney grow there on trees, but there are some to be found. That includes Ireland, which has produced a number of ex-students who have tried their hand in the English leagues. Just looking at the outside backs, the names of Carl du Chenu, Gavin Gordon and, most recently at the Sheffield Eagles and now the University of Gloucestershire All Golds, Tim Bergin, spring to mind. On top of that, any number of English students with Irish heritage have worn the green shirt with pride.

Carney believes that you have to be realistic about the chances of many students making the professional grade. 'It's a huge step up,' he says. 'And I fear for the All Golds when they come into the league. Good luck to them, but it's a big ask.'

Carney is qualified to have opinions on student teams playing in external competitions. His alma mater, UCD, fields football and rugby union teams in national competitions. 'I hope Gloucester can make a go of it,' he says. 'But I have my doubts.'

What is not in doubt is that Ireland's thriving domestic competition owes much to the spadework of Brian Corrigan and the in-put of players who have been through the Irish Students mill. 'There is definitely a place for rugby league in Ireland,' he says. 'Not for a professional club, not in my lifetime, but a real niche of its own.' It is largely the students who have carved that niche.

12. International Relations:
Today Trent Poly, Tomorrow the World

At first glance, the most remarkable thing about the Great Britain squad that flew to New Zealand for the first Student World Cup in 1986 was that it included four players from a polytechnic in a city which has always been, at best, a rugby league backwater. But Nottingham, in Trent Poly's hey-day, was a uniquely lively backwater.

Rugby league, at what is now Nottingham Trent University, was kicked off in 1982 by Gary Leadbetter and Tim Burton (not the film-maker). Within four years and without the obvious natural advantages enjoyed by some of their opponents, they had become the top student team in the country. It is hard to look back on that achievement now without asking 'How the hell did they do that?'

Part of the answer to that starts with John Yarker. A pre-Cougars Keighley supporter from Skipton, he went to Trent to take his diploma in Education. He became aware of stirrings of rugby league activity when the nascent club was having the usual problems over pitches and recognition. 'I was embarking on a career in student politics, so I thought it would be a good thing to get involved with,' he recalls. He did more than get involved; apart from playing when needed, he organised the side through its halcyon years. He can't remember having a title. 'I was just the bloke who does things.'

Trent played a couple of friendlies early in 1982 and joined the UCARLA competition later that year, under the coaching of the former Leeds University player, Rob Simpson. At the end of that season, they reached the final of the British Polytechnics Sports Association Cup, losing narrowly to Leeds Poly. Things really started to kick on, however, with an influx of northern players, headed by the Warringtonian forward, Peter Astley, and the recruitment of Mike Penistone as coach.

'What he achieved was remarkable,' says Yarker. 'He could relate really well to the players, but he could keep that bit of distance that you need. He was ahead of his time.'

Under Penistone, Trent played not only in their student competitions, but also in an East Midlands merit league. That was MANARLA - the Mansfield and Nottingham Amateur Rugby League Association - not to be confused with MASWARLA - the Midland and South-West Amateur Rugby League Association, which was a Lionel Hurst project. 'They had the money and we didn't,' is the way Yarker remembers it. MANARLA, though, served the familiar purpose of toughening-up student players, even relatively battle-hardened ones like Astley.

That little pocket of league activity was connected with the ill-fated launch in 1984 of the Mansfield Marksmen as a professional club on the Fulham/Carlisle model of ground-sharing with an established football club. They did not last long before being transformed into Nottingham City, but Mansfield-area amateur clubs at Clipstone Colliery and Garibaldi proved more durable. They also proved something of a culture shock. Astley recalls arriving at Clipstone for a match and being greeted by a baying mob of villagers, some of whom were waving a banner reading: 'Kill the Stewdents!' And he swears that was the way it was spelt. 'We didn't hang around for long afterwards,' he says.

Partly thanks to experiences like that, Trent became what Yarker calls 'quite a hard, physical team.' Penistone, who had also been coaching rugby union in Nottingham, brought across a couple of high-class players from that game in Kieran Murphy and Simon Marshall and the mix was more or less complete. The Trent Legends website calls 1985-86 the Year of the Invincibles and that is not much of an exaggeration. Trent swept all before them, culminating in a Championship final win over Hull University at Thrum Hall in Halifax. Those who saw them in their pomp reckoned that they were as good a student side as Britain had produced at that stage.

In the nature of these things, it was all very short-lived. 'You felt you really were part of something special,' says Yarker. 'But then three or four key players left.' Continuity is the hardest quality to sustain in student teams, because, by and large, players are available for three years and then leave. Trent Poly had an additional disadvantage, in that a lot of their students spent their third year working in industry, which could be anywhere in the country. Penistone 'saw the writing on the wall,' according to Yarker, and decamped to Cambridge and a dual-code coaching career that included several seasons in charge of Eastern Suburbs RU in Sydney.

The Trent Poly success story, in which he played one of the pivotal roles, was probably always destined to be a fleeting experience, which is not to underestimate what they have done since. They had a good side again in the early 90s, including the prop Tony Bowes, who went on to play first-team at Doncaster and Super League with Huddersfield, and Kevin Rudd, who played for just about everybody else. 'A man who has played for more teams and countries than anyone known in the history of rugby league,' is the way their potted history describes him.

Since then, Nottingham Trent University has maintained its presence in the middle ranks of student teams, they have a thriving alumni organisation, the aforementioned Trent Legends, who are wheeled out to take on the current crop every year. There is also an annual East Midlands 'varsity' match against Nottingham University - one of a number of rivalries around the country to have been built on the still influential Oxbridge model. They have had a good deal to do with keeping the game alive in the city and there is a considerable overlap with the Nottingham Outlaws, the amateur club who now play at the Harvey Haddon Stadium, which used to be home to the (barely) professional Nottingham City.

So they certainly play their part, but for their high-water mark you have to go back to 1986, to that unlikely Championship triumph and those four players on the plane to the inaugural World Cup in New Zealand. Along with Peter Astley and the two union converts, Kieran Murphy and Simon Marshall, there was Trevor Oates, a West Countryman who Yarker says is still the strongest prop he has ever seen, at any level. There was also Mike Penistone, although under tragic circumstances. The national Students' and Keighley coach, Geoff Peggs, had died suddenly, Mick McGowan, from the British Polytechnics set-up, was promoted in his place and Penistone appointed his assistant. They did not fly out without confidence, because they had finally beaten France at Chiswick a few weeks earlier. They flew out to Auckland with the Indonesian national carrier, Garuda. I remember them well as the cheapest way to get to Australasia in the 1980s, but they were certainly not the quickest. With a spot of crop-spraying in Sumatra, it took 30-odd hours.

Astley remembers the French arriving as fresh as daisies in the presidential jet, although his memory could be exaggerating slightly on that last detail. He also recalls the squad being accommodated 20 miles from the centre of Auckland 'in the middle on nowhere.' He might have had fonder memories if Great Britain had been more successful, but they lost 14-8 to France, 12-4 to Australia and 28-12 to the eventual winners, hosts and driving forces behind the concept, New Zealand, beating only Papua New Guinea. Sounds just like a proper World Cup.

Only one Brit, the winger, Henry Sharp, who was to go on to a good professional career at Leeds, Halifax and Rochdale, won selection in the team of the tournament, the World Student XIII, alongside Kiwis like Howie Tamati and Tea Ropati. Their 'reward' was a fixture against a President's XIII, including Gary Mercer, Shane Horo, two Manns, George and Duane, and a half-back pairing of Dave Watson and Gary Freeman! They didn't beat them.

A bigger concern than that selection was the rumbling issue of what constituted a student. It's a running theme; our boys are students, your boys are, more than likely, pseudents. Or, as the tour manager, Martyn Sadler, put it: 'The Kiwis seemed to define qualification as extending to anyone who had ever been to college. We, on the other hand, took out a side that was drawn exclusively from the student competition. We weren't prepared to consider anyone who wasn't a bona fide regular student player, and we rejected approaches from several professional stars ... in order to give an opportunity to the students who played week in, week out. I remain convinced that that is the right approach and is why we have had so much growth in the competition in the years that followed.'

Although it was a disappointing tournament from a British point of view, it did see two decisions that were significant for the future. World Cups were to be staged every three years, to fit in with the length of the average degree, and the next one would be in England. In 1989, the holders, New Zealand were the logical favourites, but the competition, based at York, had a very different look to it. Great Britain was split up into England, Ireland, Scotland and Wales - just as the senior game is, controversially, these days - and the newcomers, Holland, were added to the mix. It was not exactly the United Nations, but it was, at the time, the biggest-ever gathering of rugby league-playing countries, in one place at one time.

Rugby League in the Netherlands was a new phenomenon and heavily dependent on a student base. It was also one of those operations built upon the demented enthusiasm of one man. Mario Majone in Venice and Mike Mayer in Madison, Wisconsin, are other examples that spring to mind. In Holland, it was Hans Modderman, who got the bug whilst living in Hull and playing for Ace Amateurs and returned home determined to get his fellow countrymen playing the game.

In 1988, they did. Hull University - who else? - travelled over on the ferry to provide the opposition and beat a team called Drechstreek 46-32 in the small town of Papendrecht. It was 1994 before Holland played a full international - with students from Amsterdam and Groningen prominent - and they have had a patchy history since. Back in 1989, however, they were present and correct, with their orange tracksuits and formidable thirsts, at the World Cup, based in York.

Trevor Gibbons, who had refereed that inaugural match in Papendrecht, contributed the chapter on Holland, imaginatively titled 'Very Flat,' to the book *XIII Worlds*. This was how he described their impact: 'They certainly looked the part, dazzling the crowds with their orange shirts and the quality of their play, and they became a leitmotif for the whole tournament.'

No, the Dutch didn't actually win a match, but their stand-off and captain, Joost Takken, was named 'Top Personality' of the tournament and they attracted plenty of favourable comment with their wholehearted effort. A New Zealand report, for instance, quotes their manager-coach, the legendary Cec Mountford, as saying: 'Holland played very well and were unlucky not to score more points in the first half. We only led 18-6 at half-time and it wasn't until midway through the second half that we really took over.'

The Kiwis won 50-16, with a hat-trick of tries from Andrew Chalmers, later to head up the NZRL, but it was not to be their tournament. They drew with France in the group stages and lost their quarter final at Doncaster 20-10 to England. 'We thought we had a great chance of winning it that year, because we had a really good team that year,' recalls David Oxley, by then the chairman of the SRL. Unfortunately, as so often at so many levels, so did Australia, coached by Bill Gardner, who also had a stint in charge at Sheffield. They beat England 10-5 in the final, in front of a big crowd - claimed in some quarters to be 10,000, but actually more like 3000 - at Wigan, the vital try coming from Kurt Wrigley, later a first-grader with Cronulla, St George and Adelaide.

If that was a memorable event, then so was the end-of-tournament celebration up the road at Park Hall, beside the Camelot theme park. I say memorable, but, like the 1960s, few people who were there will actually remember very much of it, although I do have vague recollections of the French squad doing the conga, Toulouse Lautrec-style, on their knees, around the venue. Among their number was a young centre named David Fraisse, who went on to have a prolific time with Sheffield, Featherstone and the full French international side, until he had a nasty accident on his motorbike.

The Lady Mayor of Wigan was so moved by the sight of the Dutch in their traditional footwear that she gave an exhibition of her own considerable clog-dancing expertise, to great acclaim.

'A good time was had by all,' wrote the tournament organiser, Bev Risman, some years later. 'My final memory of a memorable event was rounding up the dregs who had missed their transport and throwing them in the back of the Bedford van, with all the World Cup paraphernalia for the last trip back to York.'

The unassuming Aussies had a question. 'How do you top such an effort?' their report to the game's International Board asked. 'Obviously - come to Australia.' In 1992, that was exactly what they did.

The story of that World Cup was the rise of the Pacific Nations, with Tonga, Samoa and Fiji all making their mark. Primarily, they made their mark on England, who were beaten by Fiji and drew with Samoa in the group stages. They were just softening them for the Tongans, who thrashed them 44-20 in the quarter-finals. Tonga beat New Zealand to go all the way to the final at Parramatta, where they were finally brought down to earth by a 32-14 defeat by Australia, whose future Salford utility back, Paul Carige, was one of the stars of the tournament. In the best 'one step forward, one step back' tradition of rugby league, there was no French presence, because they had no funding to make the trip.

By far the best European effort came from Clive Griffiths' Welsh squad. They beat Samoa and Fiji on their way to the semi-finals, where they met the immovable object of Australia. If that was a disappointing exit, Griffiths was able to be philosophical with hindsight. 'The players could all feel proud of their efforts, as in reality it was two colleges (Cardiff and Swansea) against two states (NSW and Queensland).' For Cardiff, read UWIC, who had by this time established themselves as a real force in the SRL. When you look at it like the Welsh coach, it really was a remarkable effort.

Peter Corcoran's report to the International Board comes across as pretty pleased with itself, as well.

'Matches were hard, fast and skilful from start to finish, played in a tremendous spirit which earned the praise of all. And, of course, played in such beautiful weather. "Games at home were never like this," chorused the visitors from the northern hemisphere - more accustomed, as they were, to cold, rain, snow and even hail.'

It had been a hugely significant tournament for the Pacific island nations, represented for the first time in a global competition. Perhaps their immediate success should not be regarded as surprising, in view of the quality of the players they had available. Fiji, for instance, had Joe Dakuitoga, later to join the Sheffield Eagles, and Livai Nalagilagi, who was to captain his country in the full World Cup in 1995. Samoa fielded Willie Swann, destined for the full international side and for Warrington. Tonga were orchestrated by Willie Wolfgramm, later to sign for Swinton.

The 1992 Student World Cup was the first indication of how important Pacific islanders were to become on the wider rugby league stage. With hindsight, it might have always been likely that they were to play a big part in the game, both on their islands of origin, in their adopted homes in New Zealand and Australia and on the other side of the world, but it was far from obvious then.

Now Polynesian players are the game's biggest growth area, in more ways that one. There are so many of them, as a quick survey of the playing fields of Auckland and Sydney will confirm. It is also an observable fact that they grow bigger, younger than the rest of humanity. That means that, whilst they can certainly look after themselves at the top level, they are even more dominant at school, youth and tertiary levels. As we will see, Student World Cups can be dominated by players of a very different physical stamp, but the 1992 tournament constituted advance notice of the general direction the game was taking.

In 1996, the event attracted a major sponsor for the first time, in the shape of the Halifax Building Society, an institution which, despite its local roots, had been strangely reluctant to get involved with the professional game. A 12-team format saw Japan, Russia, the USA and South Africa make their first appearances. The Japanese were a particularly heroic presence, in view of the life bans being handed out in that country for what the tournament programme called 'going against the grain' - ie. defying the Japanese Rugby Union.

The former Canterbury first-grader, Max Mannix, was fired by a conviction that the Japanese would be physically better suited to league than union. That theory remains unproven, but in 1996 they suffered some predictably heavy defeats. The other newcomers all had their moments of glory, however, with victories over under-performing home nations. The United States beat Ireland, Wales lost to both Russia and South Africa and, in the bowl competition South Africa beat both England and Scotland. Australia beat a typically physical Samoan side in the final at The Willows.

The 1999 World Cup is the one that induces the warm

glow on this side of the computer screen, because it was that year I badgered the *Independent* into sponsoring the tournament. That was made possible by the surprising fact that the *Indy* was a colossally league-friendly organisation at the time, edited as it was then by Simon Kelner, like his equally eminent brother, Martin, a mad-keen Swinton fan, brought up on the terraces at Station Road (I don't mean literally; they had rather a nice house in Whitefield). He used to urge me to be more unequivocal in my scepticism about Super League, until one day he had lunch with Maurice Lindsay and emerged into the sunlight as a true believer.

Anyway, the *Indifferent*, as I now think of it, threw the equivalent of a few of those lunches into the pot and the 1999 World Cup happened. It was a genuinely good fit, because the *Indy* in those days enjoyed healthy sales on campus - right up there with *Viz* and the *Sport*. The tournament was an ambitious affair, with pools - not groups, mind you - based in Paris, Cardiff, Glasgow and Belfast/Dublin.

One of my abiding memories of it all is of an endless round of motorway journeys in the company of the British Students' coach, Vinny Webb. The other is of the most exciting unknown player I've ever seen.

New Zealand's Channarith Ly was the polar opposite of the bigger-is-better, survival of the strongest philosophy that rules the rugby league roost at present. The Cambodian-born scrum-half was variously described as 5ft4, 5ft2 and 5ft. When I asked him, he wasn't sure. It would have taken three of him to make one serviceable Samoan, but one thing for certain - he could play the game. He was a nightmarishly elusive player, fast and brave, and he was the undisputed star turn of the tournament. He was instrumental in the Kiwis beating Australia in the semi-final and then he scored two tries against England in the final at The Boulevard. It wasn't a bad English side either; it included that lower division points machine, Mick Nanyn, and others who went on to have good professional careers, like Mark Sibson and Kevin Mannion. They could do nothing with Ly, however.

After he was voted player of the tournament in a landslide, the RL Alumni website concluded confidently that 'he will, in all probability, be a New Zealand star of the future at professional level.'

It never happened. Channarith Ly - the man with the biggest imbalance between his first and second names in the history of rugby league - made it as far as the reserve grade side at what was then the Auckland Warriors, but he never cracked the top team. I bet if you ask them they would say he was too small. The last reference I can find to him is playing for the Windsor Wolves in the back-blocks of Sydney, alongside some familiar faces to British fans, like Jason Chan and Dave Armitstead.

I was touched to see that he is still, in one sense, being sponsored by the *Independent* - although now the *Hawkesbury and District Independent*. I hope that they have had at least one rugby league writer prepared to drool over his miniaturised skills. He's certainly in my All-Time Student XIII; the number seven shirt, a very small one, is reserved for him. And he is surely the founder member of the Cambodian Rugby League Hall of Fame.

As for Webb, he looks back on his time coaching students as the most enjoyable of his whole career. 'But it's challenging,' he says, 'because they will question things. They will say "Why are we doing it that way? Shouldn't we try it this way instead?"'

That approach doesn't always work in other settings, he admits. When he was put in charge of the BARLA Great Britain team in the Emerging Nations World Cup, he found he had to adapt again. His assistant, from the mainstream of the amateur game, came to him and said 'The players can't cope with this. They want to be told what to do, when to do it, where to do it and how to do it.'

That is why Webb, now the RFL's head of coach development, has some words of advice for aspiring coaches. 'If they want to develop as coaches, I tell them to coach students,' he says. 'They make you question what you do and why you do it.' His estimate is that 45 per cent of the coaches in the game came through the student ranks. 'It's about planting that little seed in a lot of intelligent people's heads,' he says.

If he has one regret when he looks at it now is that the old tradition of current referees coaching sides has now all but disappeared. 'I think they're encouraged now to keep to themselves and not get involved with other aspects of the game. I think that's a shame.'

The World Cup has continued to provide a unique portal into the game for players and teams of unlikely origins. The 2005 tournament, however, was more a case of re-packaging previous participants. Instead of separate Fijian, Tongan and Samoan sides, they pooled their resources under the banner of the Pacific Islands. They proved to be rather less than the sum of their parts in the group matches, losing to England and France before thumping Wales to win the Shield. In the main final, New Zealand beat Australia by 17-8.

In 2008, the novelty value was provided by the international debut of Greece. A team shored up by Australians of Greek extraction - of whom there are more than a few - were far from being a bunch of naïve exotics. They beat Ireland and France in the group stages and went on to win the Plate. For the second time, England were runners-up, losing to Australia in the final.

Lest we conclude, though, that our student sides are

doomed to follow forever in the footsteps of their senior equivalents by never beating the Aussies in a tournament or series for 40 years or more, it should be noted that Britain won the three-match Academic Ashes series in 2011. In their 24-man squad, there were no less than ten players from the club that had come to dominate English student rugby league - Leeds Met Carnegie.

Above: Leeds University v General Accident at Soldiers Field, Roundhay, Leeds, in November 1967

Right: Leeds University v West Yorkshire Foundry at Soldiers Field in March 1967.

Below: Leeds Uni v Johnson Radley at Hunslet's Station Moor, January 1968

Above: Salford University v Sheffield University in the 1971-72 UCARLA Final at the Willows, Salford. The anxious benches look on

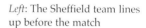

Left: The Sheffield team lines up before the match

Right: Winners Salford pose for their post-game photograph. *Below*: Action from the game. Lionel Hurst looks on

Above: Referee Fred Lindop was hugely important to student RL development

Above: Early student pioneers faced some tough challenges. Here, Leeds University face Wakefield side Stanley Rangers in November 1969

Right: Leeds v Liverpool on Leigh Rec, Widnes, in 1968, the first ever inter-University match

Above & below: Lancashire Universities and Yorkshire Universities line up at Craven Park, Hull, before the student war of the roses clash in the early 1970s

Above: Action from Scotland v Wales at Knowsley Road, St Helens, in 1988

Left: The Welsh front row giving off a traditionaly distinctive Wales front row vibe!

Below: Scotland get their hands on the ball but ultimately go down fighting

Above: Ireland face Australia in the 1989 World Cup at Knowsley Road, St Helens...

Right: ...and are watched by fellow competitiors the Scotland Students

Below: A familiar face - future professional coach Dave Rotheram in World Cup action for England

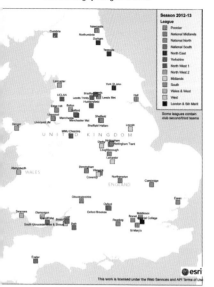

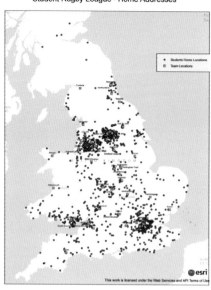

Above: Two maps showing the impressive national spread of student rugby league

Left: England take on Scotland in the 1989 World Cup

Below: Wales clear against England at the South Glamorgan Institute in 1990

Above: Brian Carney evades Clinton Toopi as Great Britain - and Ireland! - meet New Zealand in the 2005 Gillette Tri-Nations at Galpharm Stadium, Huddersfield

Right: Andy Raleigh crosses for a Wakefield try in 2011

Below: Jimmy Keinhorst troubles Warrington in the Wembley Challenge Cup final

Pics: rlphotos.com

13. Meteorology:
How Torchwood Changed the Climate...

By its very nature, student team sport tends to be cyclical. On average, a third of your squad leave every year and there is a constant process of rebuilding - sometimes successful, sometimes not. Last year's freshers are next year's gnarled veterans. Under those circumstances it should not be surprising that student rugby league in Britain should have produced not one dominant side, but a series of them.

As the early pacesetters, Leeds University could claim to be the strongest organisation in the formative years. Since then, Sheffield, Liverpool - whose run of five titles in the early 80s was the previous best - Salford, Trent and Cardiff Institute (under their various names) have all had periods during which they have set the standard.

Liverpool deserve a special mention at this stage, because their period of ascendancy also included the strange little interlude of the John Player Amateur Sevens. For two seasons, the fag-pedlars promoted this competition, in the form of a series of curtain-raisers for John Player ties proper. In 1980-1, the second of those years, Liverpool University amazed everyone by reaching the final. On the way, they beat big-guns in the amateur game, like Hull Dockers, Dudley Hill, Egremont and Leigh Miners. BARLA's Maurice Oldroyd called them 'a revelation.' Even in the final, at Wigan's Central Park, they only lost in extra-time to West Hull, who, under their previous name of Cawoods, had beaten Halifax in a Cup-tie three years earlier. The only snag was that the Uni team was what the *Rugby Leaguer*'s columnist, Keith Macklin, called 'chary of publicity,' because some of them played rugby union as well and feared being banned.

It illustrated, Macklin said, 'the iniquity of the system... It is appalling that the slightest cloud should hover over their success.' It also illustrated the way that student sides were already capable of competing with the best you could put in front of them and, 15 years after their first run-in with the rugby union border guards, briefly made Liverpool University a cause célèbre once more. Sheffield University made less of an impact, going out in the first round to INL of York, but the presence of two teams of students in a high-profile competition was a reminder to the outside world that universities were playing the game.

For cross-over potential, there has been nothing, however, remotely like Leeds Met.

Leeds Metropolitan University has its roots in an early 19th century Mechanics' Institute. It became Leeds Polytechnic and, in 1992, the city's second university. Old school cynics will say that everything with a blackboard was becoming a university around that time and since. Indeed, the slightly sniffy attitude of the established universities towards the new boys, balanced by a certain chippiness on the part of the interlopers, is a theme which has never left higher education - and which extends far beyond the rugby pitch, but can find its expression there as well as anywhere.

Along the way, rather in the manner of a snowball rolling downhill, it absorbed a number of other institutions, notably Carnegie College of Physical Education in 1976; hence the shorthand for its present identity - Leeds Met Carnegie. As soon as it acquired the second part of the name, it was part of what can be regarded as a global empire of sorts, one based on the wealth and philanthropy of one Andrew Carnegie.

Originally from Dunfermline, he emigrated to the United States and pretty much established the American steel industry, becoming in the process the second richest man in the world, after John D. Rockefeller. Carnegie was a believer in putting something back and he did not mind seeing his name chiselled above the door to prove it. Most memorably, he built hundreds of libraries in Britain and the United States, as places where working men could improve their minds. Many of the buildings currently being closed down because of cuts in funding were originally Carnegie libraries.

Then there was Carnegie Hall, still the most iconic performance venue in New York and the subject of a classic Big Apple joke. 'How do I get to Carnegie Hall?' a newcomer is alleged to have asked a New Yorker, who replied: 'Practice, buddy, practice.' You could say the same about getting into the Leeds Met first team.

Carnegie once offered $20 million to the Philippines, to buy their independence from the USA, because he disapproved of American imperialism. Nevertheless, his own empire survived him. It was a grant from the Carnegie Trust that financed the opening of the PE College in 1933, long after his death, and it earned a reputation for sporting excellence long before it came under the Leeds Met umbrella.

In the 21st century, however, it has become a brand. In rugby league alone, the Carnegie name has been attached to the Challenge Cup and the World Club Challenge. For a time, they were majority shareholders in the Leeds Tykes rugby union club, or Leeds Carnegie as they were at this stage.

Headingley - sorry, Headingley Carnegie - is now in effect an extra campus, with facilities that are used by the university. On the other hand, the RFL's full-time referees are based at the original campus, up the road at Becketts Park, where they spend far too much time in each other's company. Just for a bit of variety, Carnegie also sponsored Irish football and the Northern Ballet Theatre. They also have a branch campus at Bhopal in India. Yes, the Bhopal of the clouds of poison gas; well, it would be, wouldn't it? I turned on the telly recently and the Chennai Super Kings were playing Yorkshire Carnegie.

The man behind this bulging portfolio of outside interests was Professor Simon Lee. He once explained his philosophy to me and it was one of a marketplace where only the fittest and most energetic survive. At a time of competition for students, his key role was to make sure that Leeds Met's profile was so high that it won that competition. It was the epitome of education as a business; a long, long way from the Mechanics' Institute.

The joke at the time was that, if you left anything lying around, Carnegie would pounce and sponsor it. The way they appeared to have tentacles everywhere reminded me of something - apart from Andrew Carnegie's business empire. I had not watched *Doctor Who* regularly since hiding behind the settee from the Daleks, but my grand-daughter is a bit of a fan. Watching it with her introduced me to *Torchwood*, the shadowy organisation that later got a series of its own. Basically, it was the unseen power that controlled everything. Carnegie was heading in that direction. The clue, apparently, is in the name; *Torchwood* is an anagram of *Doctor Who*. The anagram of Carnegie is Eager Inc. For a while, they were eagerness itself and were all over rugby league like a rash, with eager, smiley-faced students around every corner. It was a bit like being welcomed to a game by the Moonies, but, my word, you certainly knew who Leeds Met Carnegie were.

There were those with qualms over how all this profile-building had been financed and in 2009, amid allegations of the misuse of funds, Prof. Lee resigned as vice-chancellor. The university divested itself of its 51 per cent of the Tykes and became a reluctant partner in its Challenge Cup sponsorship, earning the undying enmity of certain strata of journalists by doing away with the pre-Cup final piss-up. Everything written about them should be read with that in mind. The following year, Radio 4's *Face the Facts* got stuck in, which is rarely good news for its subjects. The Rottweiler of the Airwaves went for the jugular, but Prof. Lee fought his corner, remaining unrepentant and insisting that all would have been well if he had been left to get on with it. He was able to point to success in maintaining the level of applications as evidence of a job well done.

Despite that, it was farewell, Prof. Lee. Or was it just au revoir? One recurring characteristic of rugby league is that, when someone crashes and burns, the first thing you wonder is where they are going to show up next. The answer in this case is Oxford, although that is a little further down the track. Meanwhile, back at Leeds Met, the symbiotic relationship with the game seems to have survived the upheavals. The university is proud of its rugby league links and uses them as a selling point in its prospectus. In its selected list of alumni, it includes the singer and gay icon, Marc Almond, the jailed architect, John Poulson, and Kevin Sinfield, who between them cover most bases.

'If you want to play rugby league to a high standard, Leeds Met is the place for you,' it says. 'Many players have graduated from Leeds Met and gone on to work within the game, either for the clubs direct, or for the governing body, the RFL.' And some have gone on to play professionally, like Neil Cherryholme at Keighley, Vinny Finegan at Bradford, Alex Scott at Batley and Halifax's Rob Worrincy, the most unpredictable and sometimes most brilliant winger in the Championship. If anything, he was even more so as a student. Paul Fletcher recalls one match when, the first three times he touched the ball, he knocked-on. The next two, he scored length-of-the-field tries.

The most intriguing names, because we do not yet know how good they could turn out to be, are those of Jimmy Keinhorst and Alex Walmsley. At the other end of their playing careers, Adrian Morley and Jamie Peacock both plan to study Sports Administration at Leeds Met when they finally hang up their boots. I can already hear the sigh of relief that accompanies their assurances that they do not intend to play as students. That might just be too steep a learning curve for an unsuspecting student front-row.

The current Leeds first-teamer, Ian Kirke, is taking his MBA there and decided against a move to Wakefield, at least in part because he wasn't sure how well his rugby would fit in with his studies if he was at another club. As for Sinfield, he plans to add a Leeds Met MA to his qualifications. Throw in the names of two candidates for the title of Leeds' greatest player of all time, Eric Harris ('The Toowoomba Ghost') and Lewis Jones, both of whom passed through Carnegie, and it is clear that the connections go very deep.

The Met's head coach, Paul Fletcher, is further evidence of that. He firmly believes he has 'the best job in rugby league. I get to work with young athletes and improve them, not just as rugby players, but as people.' Fletcher believes unapologetically in rugby league's ability to do just that - and he should know. Since a playing career as a versatile utility back for Leeds, he has proved to be an equally versatile coach. His CV includes spells in charge of Bramley and Gateshead and as assistant at the Rhinos, but his greatest input and impact has been at student level.

Fletcher made 120 first-team appearances in nine seasons as a player at Headingley, in competition with the likes of Les Dyl and John Holmes, with the latter of whom he had been at school. 'I soon realised that I had to work twice as hard to be half as good,' he says now. It's odd how that formula is so frequently a qualification for success, further down the track, as a coach in many sports. He was never a star. 'I was just proud to be part of that team.'

For almost as long, he was part of the slightly less glamorous team at Bramley and it was there, at the suggestion of the then coach, Maurice Bamford, that he got his first taste of coaching. That was with the local district development side; kids in many cases with little structure or discipline in their lives whom he turned into a team and five of whom became professionals. His route into student rugby league was through the back door. He took over as coach of the amateur club, Milford, and soon realised that they needed new blood. In a flash of inspiration, he wondered whether there might be students in the city who fancied a game at weekends. He approached the then Leeds Met coach, Peter Roe, recruited a few likely lads and turned a declining club around.

Because of that link, Fletcher was already on the Met radar when Roe resigned. The most productive partnership between coach and institution in the history of the student game was forged. Leeds Met were by no stretch of the imagination a dominant force at that level when he arrived in 1998.

'We were in danger of relegation. The good teams were Liverpool John Moores, St Mary's, Northumbria, UWIC of course and still, at that time, Leeds Uni.' In his first game in charge, they were beaten by John Moores, but relegation was avoided and the juggernaut that was to be Leeds Met was ready to rumble. In the next three seasons, they beat UWIC in three Grand Finals and became unarguably the best in the game.

How was this achieved? The easy answer is by throwing money and resources at the competition. The English Students tour brochure for the 2005 World Cup spelt out the difference between the Met and the rest:

'Leeds Metropolitan University has introduced the Carnegie Sports Scholarship Scheme that gives scholars the opportunity to develop their sporting performance alongside the pursuit of academic studies. This will be achieved by providing general, technical and financial support. In addition, each scholar is allocated a sports mentor...' The attraction, back in those carefree days, was pretty obvious. The reality these days, as we shall see, is rather different.

In 2002, Paul took his own version of a gap year, or a gap couple of years. Part funded by Leeds Rhinos, he was seconded to Gateshead, or what remained of Gateshead after the Long March to Hull, with instructions to 'steady the ship.' It was a very different experience. 'I'd been used to winning, but soon after I got there we played Salford and lost 90-8 - and we were playing them again the next week. I didn't know what to say to them in that situation.' He consulted a sports psychologist, who advised the setting of small goals. Gateshead lost 100-12, so at least they could claim to have slightly improved their goalkicking. He shored up the team with students from the University of Northumbria - with whom there is still an overlap - and the occasional Rhinos loanee, like Ryan Bailey. The ship was not exactly steadied, but it did not sink either and the way that it remains perilously afloat to this day is one of rugby league's little miracles.

Fletcher took up the reins again at Leeds Met in 2004, riding a wave of success that has continued for eight unbroken years, after a transitional first season which started with a 30 point defeat by Leeds University - provocatively identified by their forward, Dave Norcross, in the 2005 World Cup brochure as 'proper Leeds.' Six weeks later, the Met went to their place and beat them.

Since then, they have won seven consecutive Grand Finals, all against the unfortunate Loughborough. Their record in student competitions over that length of time reads lost 3, drawn 2, won 161. Those five games they have failed to win still seem to be imprinted on his mind. Going back to any of the locations feels to him like going back to the scene of a death in the family, he says. They have reached the first round proper of the Challenge Cup five times, beating opposition of the calibre of Wigan St Pats to get there. In 2012, not just were the first team unbeaten, but the 'A'-team as well. It is a record of dominance of St George or Wigan proportions and it is appropriate that we should be talking next to the trophy cabinet at Carnegie, groaning as it is with silverware. Not all the trophies are for rugby league, but an awful lot are and the same is true of another cabinet at the other end of the café.

Ah yes, I hear every other team in the land say, but they shell out for all the best players and treat them like full-time professionals. They should win everything. There is a germ of truth in that. They are able to offer superb facilities and professional coaching. What they do not have, since the Simon Lee meltdown, is the cash for any up-front scholarships.

'I never offer anyone a scholarship,' says Fletcher. 'What I do tell them is, that if they apply themselves and they do well, there could be bursaries in their second year.' That promise is enough to attract the cream of the players in the Under-19 college competition, which he and his assistant, Paul Cook, scout meticulously.

The other thing he can promise them is plenty of hard work. 'I tell them it will be hard. I don't pull the wool over their eyes. But I tell them that, if they can do it, they can have the best three years of their lives.'

What is demanded of them is a schedule like this:

Monday - weights and wrestling;

Tuesday - skills and match preparation;

Wednesday - match day;

Thursday - rehab and swimming;

Friday - sprints.

And those sprints are at 7.30 a.m.

It's impossible to visualise anything more alien to the popular picture of student life, but there were 27 at the last session before I was there. In theory, the weekends are their own, but woe betide anyone who used to get the worse for wear at that favourite student pub near the Headingley campus, the Skyrack, because Paul's wife, Carmel, used to be the landlady there. Carmel, by the way, knows all about the depth of her husband's obsession. He recalls her looking up from her book on a holiday and asking him what he was scribbling. 'I'm picking my all-time Leeds Met team,' he told her. 'You relax in your way and I'll relax in mine.'

His philosophy is quite simple. We provide you with professional facilities and professional coaching, so the least you can do is behave like professionals. That means it is not for everyone, but Fletcher says he does not kick anyone out of the squad as not good enough.

'It's hard, so if you're not getting a game, you tend to kick yourself out. If you stick at it, though, you will eventually get a game.' There are requirements away from training and playing as well. Fletch, as they are allowed to call him, is a stickler for good manners, for speaking politely for the people who serve you your meal, for instance. And, be warned, he has a particular down on wearing hats and caps indoors.

The coach is unashamedly moulding the young men in his charge. There was one time when he felt they needed a bit of toughening up - see Sheffield University and Trent Poly, among others - so he entered them in the Leeds and District Cup. As if by magic, they came out of the hat with Queens - the meanest, baddest set of mothers in West Yorkshire. The Met won the match, but lost the fight. 'Not on points either,' says Fletcher. 'By several knock-outs. But I was able to tell them they would never, ever be in a match as tough.' Thanks for that, coach.

There is another bonus that they get from having Paul Fletcher in charge. For over two decades, he has been seconding himself to incoming tours and visits, as a sort of semi-official liaison man, a gopher, he calls it, as in 'gopher this, gopher that.' He made himself so useful that Chris Anderson, when he was Australian coach, asked him what he wanted to be paid. 'I told him I didn't want any money. I just wanted to watch.' He has watched and learned from a generation of Australian coaches, with a view to applying that to his students. They have had the benefit of sessions with Wayne Bennett, to name the most legendary of the lot.

Another little side-benefit is that Leeds Met play their home games not on some windswept park pitch, but at

Headingley. When it is out of commission, as for the laying of a new pitch in the winter of 2012, they have a 3G artificial pitch of their own.

They do undeniably have a few in-built advantages, all of which raise the question of whether Leeds Met are just a bit too good for the best interests of the SRL. It's a charge with which Fletcher is familiar and to which he has some salient points to add. To start with, he points out that he does not push the selection envelope as hard as he could. During LMC's particularly publicity-hungry phase, he once came under pressure to include Barrie McDermott in the side to play Leeds Uni. 'There was no problem about his eligibility. He was a bona-fide student, but I wouldn't ask him to play. He would have frightened the life out of them, but how would you feel if you'd played all the way through and then you were dropped?

'They asked then if he could just be on for the kick-off. I told them it depended on what sort of kicking-off they had in mind - but no, it wouldn't have been the right thing to do.'

Then he recommends a closer look at their 2012 playing record. 'We didn't sweep everyone before us,' he says. 'We won four matches by four points or less and 2013 is probably the first time we've gone into a new season and not been favourites... there for the taking.' The sides he is most wary of are those eternal bridesmaids from Loughborough and the New Model Army from Gloucestershire - who actually beat the champions a couple of weeks after he issued his warning. Make no mistake about it, Leeds Met will still have a good side - propped up, Fletcher says, by a particularly strong intake over the last couple of years from Oldham - but the days of trampling everyone underfoot could be coming to an end. Or maybe it's his way of psyching himself up and avoiding any complacency.

He takes pleasure not only in the future professionals

who have come through his system, but also in the dozen or more - another holiday list, perhaps - who are in positions of influence within the game, from Featherstone to Fiji. 'But do you know what really pleases me? It's when someone I've coached invites me to his wedding. If, years later, they do that, I must have had some influence on them.' Maybe, in a lot of cases, that promise of the best three years of their lives was not so far from the mark.

For all the talent that has passed through his hands, neither Paul Fletcher nor any other student coach has ever had two players at his disposal who have made their mark quite like Walmsley and Keinhorst did in 2012. Neither of them, though, came through the normal channels.

At 16, Walmsley gave up the game he had played as a kid at Dewsbury Celtic. He was not much short of the 6ft5 he stands now, but a lot heavier.

'I was very overweight and I just lost confidence,' he says now. It was a coach at Celtic, Paul Heaton, who coaxed him back a couple of years later and showed him the benefits of getting himself fit. Meanwhile, Alex was starting a degree in Quantity Surveying at Leeds Met, but playing for his club rather than his university.

When Celtic played a friendly against England Students, however, the Students' coach, one Paul Fletcher, discovered that the big prop who was doing all the damage was a Leeds Met lad! Not surprisingly, he was determined to get him on board for his third and final year - and his progress since then has been startling. He starred in the side that won their seventh BUCS title in as many years, was named the SRL Player of the Year and earned himself a trial at that progressive little Yorkshire club, Batley. 'I tipped off Leeds,' says Fletcher. 'They came and had a look, but thought he was a bit too old.' So Batley it was - and that proved to be an alternative route into Super League.

'John Kear sat me down and told me that they were going to take a chance on me,' he says. 'I was expecting to play a few games here and there. But apart from a couple of games I missed when I had a knock, I played every one.'

Not only that, he waltzed off with a clutch of club awards, plus the coveted title of Championship Young Player of the Year. Somehow, in the middle of all this, he managed to get a 2:1 in Quantity Surveying. 'It was hectic at times,' he says, 'but I've had quite a year.' It wasn't over yet. A little later, he had to make what he describes as a difficult phone call to his prospective employers, telling them that he would not after all be going to work for them, as he had signed a full-time contract with St Helens. As excuses go, it's not a bad one; and there will still be quantities to be surveyed when he's 30. 'At least, I hope there will. It's something to fall back on,' he says.

It was Saints' acting coach and former Scottish student international Mike Rush who spotted his potential. To be fair, he doesn't exactly hide it under a bushel; 6ft5, 18 stone front-rowers who can shift and don't mind dishing a bit out don't grow on trees, even in the Heavy Woollen District. Garry Schofield, who coached him on a BARLA Young Lions tour to South Africa, said that Saints had signed 'a gem' and that could be spot-on. Fletcher says he has 'a good outside chance of making an England squad.' In his style on the pitch, he reminds me of Lee Bamber, the Blackpool Borough and - briefly - Wigan prop of the early 80s, who was shot dead in a gangland revenge killing. One difference was that he didn't have a 2:1 in Quantity Surveying.

Alex is just back from his off-season weight training when we talk. It is going to be another hectic year. 'I'll just put everything else on the back-burner and concentrate on making as much progress as I can,' he says. Initially, that is likely to be back in a Batley shirt, as Saints take advantage of the dual registration system to loan him back to his previous club. At 22, he has plenty of time to make it as a regular Super League player and it is an arrangement that seems to suit all parties. 'I knew there were clubs watching me. A couple of them approached me directly, but St Helens went through the club. It's a massive step up, but I'm ready to go full-time.'

Walmsley is the joint-product of three strands of the game below Super League level: the amateurs, the students and the part-time professional community clubs. He knows what he gained from his relatively short, but undeniably spectacular stint as a student player.

'I wouldn't say it was as physical,' he says. 'It's more of a classy standard of rugby. There are some very skilful players, especially in the top two or three teams. There are players there who could make the transition to full-time football and I think professional clubs should look there more than they do.'

By way of illustration, he points to some of the early progress made by a few of his Leeds Met team-mates. His fellow-prop, Michael Sykes, originally from the St Ives Roosters in Cambridgeshire and Player of the Series in the victorious Academic Ashes campaign of 2010, has played for the London Skolars. Owain Griffiths, son of Clive, has played for him at the North Wales Crusaders and Walmsley is confident that there are others who could go as far or further.

And then, in a little category of his own, there is Jimmy Keinhorst, a young player who makes Alex's route into the professional game look deeply conventional and his progress positively pedestrian by comparison.

In 2011, he was a Sports Science undergraduate, playing a few games for the Rhinos' Under-20s, as well as for Leeds Met. By the end of 2012, he had written himself a couple of footnotes in the history of the world's oldest rugby league competition, one of which can never be taken away from him and another which is unlikely to be. When Keinhorst came on as a second-half substitute for Leeds in their Challenge Cup final defeat by Warrington, he became, in terms of previous first-team minutes, the least experienced Leeds player ever to appear in a major final, although Hull's Mike Smith made his first-team debut against Wakefield at Wembley in 1960, which is going to take some beating. Keinhorst has hardly got over the shock yet.

'There were plenty of players they could have picked who had more experience than me,' he says. 'Plus, teams don't often carry a centre on the bench.' Okay, the game was long gone by the time he got onto the pitch at Wembley and someone, someday might get the nod for a Cup final with even fewer miles on the clock. One distinction Jimmy Keinhorst can never be deprived of, however, is that he was the first German to play in the game's showpiece.

It's not so much a long story as a rather labyrinthine one, and it begins with Jimmy's dad, Wolfgang, coming to England from his hometown of Bochum in his mid-20s and never going home. He married a girl from Birmingham and has just completed 35 years teaching German at - where else? - Leeds Met. He also founded an unlikely-sounding dynasty of international rugby league players, brothers Christian, Marcus, Nick and Jimmy all having played for the fledgling German national side. It is Jimmy, though, whose career has really taken wing, even if it has not flown in a straight line.

Despite the Leeds Met connection, he originally went to university at Newcastle, but didn't take to it. That led to a sort of extended gap year, which included a spell playing rugby union in Queensland and five months doing likewise in Germany - the only five months he has ever spent in his fatherland. That doesn't prevent him being jokily typecast in the Leeds dressing room as a prototypical Teuton. 'You can't be tired,' the Leeds pack's master of the one-liner (and Leeds Met graduate) Jamie Jones-Buchanan told him after one match. 'You're German. You're built to last.' Keinhorst had an answer up his sleeve that disproves a lot that you might have suspected about German humour. 'Yes, but I'm half English,' he said, 'and that half's knackered.'

The key moment for Keinhorst was making a phone call to Paul Fletcher. 'He told me he wasn't getting a game at Otley and wanted to play league again.' Once they had him safely within the fold, Leeds Met knew they had got something a bit special. Fletcher asked the Rhinos' coaching staff to come and see him in action and the upshot was a one-year, part-time contract to play in the Under-20s.

'Even that was a massive leap up,' he says. 'To be completely honest, playing in the student league you have a couple of competitive games, against the likes of Loughborough and probably now Gloucestershire, and some that just aren't.' That's the potential problem, of course. Leeds Met, built on the American college sport model - with professional coaches and structured recruitment - rather than anything we are familiar with in this country, are just a bit too slick. 'I think Fletch is pretty good at recruiting good players for the team,' he says. With both first and second teams unbeaten in 2012, that is something of an understatement.

Inevitably, Keinhorst's focus will be elsewhere from here onwards. His initial impact at Super League level has been good enough to earn him a full-time contract for 2013-2015 and you can see how he fits into Leeds' alternative interchange strategy. A centre on the bench gives you a flexibility that a lot of teams, with four forward substitutes, have sacrificed. Brian McDermott can bring on Keinhorst, move Carl Ablett into the pack and not lose much defensively.

The first year of his Super League contract overlaps with the final year of his Sports Science degree, but he is undaunted at the prospect of combining the two. 'I think I could get a 2:1 or even a first, so I really want to go for it.'

Similar progress in his playing career would see him as a regular first-teamer. They don't mind a challenging timetable, these Leeds Met lads, but, then again, they are part of a secret organisation that runs the world.

That best-ever Leeds Met team, by the way... both of them are in it. Barrie McDermott isn't.

14. Psychology:
How Great Britain Taught Australia a Lesson

Sometimes, it looks as though student rugby league has got a few things right that the senior game is still struggling with. Take the international dimension, for instance.

The SRL has England, Scotland, Wales and Ireland teams for the home internationals, incoming tours and World Cups, but they all come together as Great Britain to play Australia for the Ashes.

In other words, it has the template that most people would like to see at full Test level, but which the RFL, ARL and International Federation have so far proved incapable of putting into place.

The Academic Ashes were instituted in 1997, largely at the instigation of Warrington-born Australian Universities coach, Mike Loftus, although it was not a smooth start. Thanks to an internal dispute in Australia - in rugby league? Surely not - New South Wales pulled out and the national team was composed entirely of Queenslanders. It didn't seem to matter too much as they won convincingly at Cheltenham and Keighley, with one Lote Tuqiri in their side. The British coach, Vinny Webb, admitted in his report that 'the obvious lack of fitness was a concern and the general lack of self-belief.'

The following year, the Lions went Down Under and lost in both Toowoomba and Brisbane.

It was the same story at Rochdale in a one-off match after the 1999 World Cup. Two players who were to become familiar to European spectators - Adam Mogg and Mitchell Sargent - were in the Aussie side. It was the first time that a trophy was presented, after a pennant from each side was ceremonially burnt and the ashes placed inside a silver urn, bearing a verse specially written by the Northern Irish poet, Patrick Maguire.

> 'Study this: In these Ashes endless rebeginning
> Friendship's phoenix rising both in losing and
> in winning
> Rendered only brighter here, through combat's
> fire and battle's flame
> Enduring joy, the world in play, the spirit free,
> the glory of our game.'

It makes the Super League Trophy, let alone the League Leaders' hub-cap seem a little prosaic.

Patrick McGuire happens to be the brother-in-law of Niel Wood, who phoned him one morning and asked him if he could knock out a verse by mid-day. It might not be his finest work, but it is his quickest.

After another one-off defeat in Brisbane in 2000, GB finally made their breakthrough the following year with a 21-8 win at Hull - or did they? Strictly speaking, it was only

Queensland they beat, inter-state hostilities having broken out again in Australia.

From 2003, Britain faced a fair dinkum full Australian side, losing two match series' away and at home that year and 2004. The closest they came was at Dewsbury in '04, when a try 13 minutes from time by Alan Robinson, now the mover and shaker at Coventry, gave our brave boys a 14-6 lead, only for the Aussies to snatch it 18-14.

By 2006, Paul Fletcher had taken over from the former Hull KR coach, Gary Wilkinson, and, although the series was again lost, two of the three defeats were by eight points apiece. They certainly didn't lose for want of thorough preparation. Each member of the squad was given a little light in-flight reading, in the shape of a 100-page dossier encompassing just about every aspect of the task ahead.

Many professional touring sides might do something similar; only the Academic Lions have one with a suggested reading list on the last page. Other delights, before you get that far, include a mission statement, the obligatory quotes from Vince Lombardi, travel hints - no alcohol, no coffee, no fizzy drinks, no resemblance to England teams going to France 30 years earlier - nutrition, injury management, John Kear on the way that 80 minutes can change your life, a play-book containing a couple of dozen set-moves, mental rehearsal and visualisation.

They might not have won the series, but they were exceptionally well-read.

In fact, Fletcher believed that they could have won all three Tests. In 2007, they lost another series, despite winning the middle Test and losing the other two by four points apiece, this time at home, and, when the Aussies came over for two Tests in 2010, they had a secret weapon up their sleeves.

'He was the oldest-looking student I've seen in my life,'

Fletcher said of the Australian stand-off, Drew Dalton. He bore an uncanny resemblance to the greatest stand-off of them all, Wally Lewis; and not Wally Lewis as he was then either, Wally Lewis as he is now. Unfortunately for Great Britain, he played a bit like Wally Lewis as he was then, especially in a 40-30 victory on the artificial pitch at Leigh East.

And so to the annus mirabilis of 2011.

Great Britain were supposed to play an Australian side in Bali, but with the memories of the bombings still fresh and Osama Bin Laden just killed, the Aussies opted out. Instead, the Lions played a Balinese XIII - fleshed out with a few expats - another first for student rugby league.

It wasn't much of a contest, but they followed it with a toughening-up exercise against the Northern Territory in Darwin. 'It had been a bit of a holiday up to then, but when we got to Darwin Fletch sat us down and told us in no uncertain terms that it was time to get serious,' Keinhorst recalls.

The Lions should have won the first Test in Brisbane, but were held to a 20-all draw. 'We were the better side and the feeling in the dressing room was that it was a point lost,' Fletcher says.

They won the second, also in Brisbane, 10-4 and went into the decider on a steamy night in Cairns quietly confident.

'We should have beaten them in one match and we'd kept them to four points in the other. We expected to win.'

Perhaps that's the first psychological requirement; the difference between innumerable British sides at all levels who sincerely believed they could beat Australia in a series or tournament and the Boys of 2011 is that the Academic Lions actually did it - and in some style, as well, winning 24-10.

'Nigel Scott's kicking game was superb, Jimmy Keinhorst scored an 80-metre try, but we dominated them in the pack,' Fletcher says.

Keinhorst himself remembers the try in slightly more modest terms. 'It was more like 60,' he says. 'But it was still a pretty decent try. I got a pass from my centre, John Paxton, that put me outside the winger. I chipped over the full-back and that was that. It was a fantastic feeling. We went out and had a few drinks, because we hadn't been allowed to do that.'

Apart from imposing that sort of discipline and rooming players with team-mates from different universities - difficult when you have a dozen from one place - Fletcher had had to juggle with a tricky selection dilemma.

He had taken his 24-man squad to Australia with the promise that they would all get a game. Before the third Test, two of them - Jordan Rice of Gloucestershire and Crawford Matthews from Hull - had still not had a run. The pragmatic thing to have done would have been to stick with a winning team, but Fletcher felt that would be in breach of his covenant with his squad. Both played - and played a full part in the victory.

'It was very, very emotional,' says Fletcher. 'The best day of my coaching career. Someone said it had been 39 years trying to win a series, so it's hard to top that.' The mathematics of that may be open to some dispute, but you get the general idea.

Equally memorable, for different reasons, was taking a Great Britain Students side to Serbia.

'The most racist place I've ever been to,' he says, an assessment that will strike a chord with any one who witnessed the scenes at the end of England's Under-21 football international in October 2012.

There were four black players in Fletcher's squad and

they were racially abused with depressing regularity; not by their opponents, it must be added, but by Mr and Mrs Average on the streets. Their white team-mates were of a mind to wade in on their behalf and an international incident was narrowly averted.

15. Philosophy:
There's More Than One Way to be a Pioneer

The other context in which the Great Britain name - brand, some would call it - survives and thrives is through the Great Britain Student Rugby League Pioneers.

They might have only existed under that slighty unwieldy name since 2005, but they represent a continuation of the touring instinct which runs through the student game like the blue through Stilton. Need a team to fly the flag in foreign parts? The obvious answer for the last 20 years has been to send a team of students. Morocco in 1994 was a good example. A Great Britain Students side was based on the waterfront at Casablanca - they actually did their training on the beach - and played and beat Morocco Students, Combined Services and the full Morocco side.

Perhaps even more memorable than that was the trip to Kazan in 2001. The capital of the Russian region of Tatarstan hosted what must rank as the most remarkable of all international rugby league tournaments. England, Scotland, Ireland and Wales were all represented individually, along with Tatarstan, Russia and New South Wales.

In Tatarstan, it was very big news indeed. 'The players were treated like pop stars,' says Gerard Keenan, the Irish team manager on that trip. 'Like Westlife or something. They had the time of their lives. Even people like me were signing autographs.'

At one stage, he was confronted by what he took to be a heavily tattooed, shaven-headed local.

'He wanted me to sign his arm, but they were both already full of signatures. In the end, I signed his head.'

So, if you're ever in Kazan and you spot a man in a vest with the words 'Gerard Keenan' across his head in felt-tip, you will know the story.

As Irish team manager, Keenan also had the unforgettable experience of leading out Ireland for the first game, in front of 17,000 spectators. They had been a little short of international competition in Tatarstan and they were, as they say, mad for it. England, featuring a young Andy Raleigh, won the tournament, but that, as ever, was only part of the object of the exercise.

When they adopted the Pioneers trademark, it was with one eye on the dictionary, where the term is defined variously thus:

1. One who is first or among the earliest in any field of inquiry, enterprise, or progress.
2. One who opens up new areas of thought, research, or development.
3. (Ecology) An animal or plant species that establishes itself in a previously barren environment.

Through a series of visits to Estonia, the Czech Republic, Latvia, Ukraine, Norway, Kazakhstan, Greece and Poland, they have lived up to all three of those definitions.

Gerard Keenan is a veteran of six of those tours. 'You get people wanting to go on jollies to Malta and Lebanon, where there is something up and running, but the idea is that we go to virgin territory. It's important that we take the right lads, who will contribute off the field as well,' he says of quite a rigorous selection process. 'I like to sit down with each of the lads and make sure they want to go for the right reasons.'

Gerard is one of those rugby league activists who wears a dazzling selection of hats. Originally from the famous nursery of the game that is Wigan St Pats, he has lived in North Wales for 20 years and has been immersed in Welsh, Irish and student rugby league. I arranged to meet him on the touchline at the Bolton versus Bangor University match, because he also coaches Bangor.

For all his tireless activity in these islands, some of his most vivid memories concern his travels with the Student Pioneers.

I doubt whether the chairman of the SRL remembers it as fondly, but one of Gerard's favourites involves John Piercy being struck down with Ukraine Belly on the night train from Kiev, with no usable toilet facilities on board. Then there was the search for a pitch in Riga, in turbulent times when people were simply grabbing land where they could. They finished up playing 50 miles out of the city on a patch of rough ground in the middle of a housing estate, marked out with sawdust.

What is more, the Pioneers had to pay £800 for that sawdust, as the Latvians showed that they were getting the hang of capitalism. In the absence or either whitewash or sawdust in Lodz, they marked out the pitch with lemons.

GB Student Pioneers: In 2012, the Pioneers returned from
a historic tour of Poland, where they took part in the first ever
game of rugby league to be staged in that country.
Coached by Lee Speight, the tourists represented
the universities of Trinity and All Saints, Manchester Met,
Northumbria, Bath, Bradford, Nottingham, Oxford,
Birmingham, Hull, Huddersfield, Swansea, UWIC,
TASC, Liverpool John Moores and Imperial
Photo: www.studentrl.com

'Often it's what happens off the pitch that's most
important,' says Keenan. 'Whenever we trained, we would
have an open training session to get the locals involved.' He
recalls giving an old ball to some boys in the Czech
Republic. Hours later and in the pitch-dark, they were still
playing in the street with it.

The most recent foray, to Poland, saw the Pioneers play
the first matches in that country, against its first rugby

league club, the Lodz Magpies. Okay, they were beaten 98-0 and 82-0, but that wasn't really the point.

'The game-time there wasn't about us flexing our superiority, but to show how the game should be played in terms of the style and spirit of the game,' wrote the UWIC hooker, Louis Singleton, who was on that trip, which ended with a match against the inaugural Polish national side, who were basically the Lodz Magpies without the cohesion and lost by an eye-watering 158-0. Everyone has to start somewhere, however, and the record of Pioneers' tours is that they have sown the seeds of rugby league pretty much wherever they have gone.

The tourists have learned a few things as well. A number of them in Poland went to Auschwitz, which Singleton described as 'one of the most moving things I've ever been a part of.' The first Pioneers' tour, to Estonia, was addressed by a concentration camp survivor.

It was in pursuit of recollections like that that I went to meet Gerard at Bolton Arena, as well as to see the student game at, with all due respect, its lower levels - North West Division 2.

What I found was that the same virtues of tolerance, humour and flexibility that are an essential part of the tour baggage are also needed closer to home.

'What I always tell them on Pioneers tours is not to expect everything to go smoothly,' Keenan says. 'If things aren't quite as we would like them, fine, we find a way round it. If we have to get back on the bus and go another 50 miles, so be it.'

The Bangor bus has been at Bolton for two hours and they have discovered that there is only a water-logged pitch with football goals still in place. Bolton have no coach and only 11 players and it's starting to rain. Some frantic phoning around gets Leigh East to agree to lend out their pitch ten miles away. So onto the bus go the Bangor squad, most of the Bolton lads, the referee, me and a couple of push-bikes. It wouldn't have surprised me to have seen a crate of live chickens and a couple of goats, such was the third world flavour of the operation.

Easts have come to the rescue before, notably in the big freeze of 2009, when everything else in the country was rock-solid and both Academic Ashes games were played on their artificial pitches. For this glamorous fixture, they happily hand over their first-team pitch, which is a) enormous and b) as smooth and manicured as Wembley. Neither of those factors help Bolton, who are more impressed than anything by the way the dressing room doors have been labelled 'Bolton University' and 'Bangor University' at ten minutes notice. I once wandered down the same corridor and found one door labelled 'Stonyhurst College,' so it is not just rugby league teams they help out.

NW2 is down to four teams following the withdrawal of Chester - who Gerard also used to coach - after unspecified atrocities during freshers' week, but they are still a disparate bunch; today's two combatants, of course, plus Manchester Uni's 'A' team and the once-mighty Lancaster. That means only three home fixtures and three away in the league, so you don't give one up lightly.

So it is that Bolton take the field with two borrowed players, no coach, no medical kit, no kicking tee and two supporters - the hooker's girl-friend and myself. Bangor, on the other hand, are a well-organised little side. They have proper, regular training sessions - an American, a Canadian and a lad from Hong Kong had turned up at the last one, apparently - and it shows. Bolton, at a generous estimate, have three players who know roughly what they're doing and the rest are raw novices, several of them playing their first-ever games.

Not surprisingly in the circumstances, they lost by plenty to not very much.

One Bangor prop drove the kick-off back at them, the other got a killer pass out of the back door. Bolton conceded their first try at the end of the second set and they were on the back foot from there on.

A couple of their players had only the woolliest of notions of how to play the ball. To his eternal credit, the referee, rather than penalise them every time, showed them how to do it and allowed them another go if they got it wrong. By this time it was bucketing it down and, when a player was injured and having treatment - mainly from Gerard - the rest sheltered in Easts' state of the art dugout.

A Bangor player came to the touchline and asked if anyone could relocate his dislocated finger. We all had a go - me, the coach driver, the bar-steward, the groundsman, the hooker's girl-friend and a couple of passing Leythers. By the time we finished, that finger looked a bit straighter, but the rest of his hand was all over the place.

Bolton deserved credit for never chucking it in and they had a few players who, with a bit of training and a bit of timing, could be quite useful. In the meantime, they had at least managed to get a game played and that seemed to be what mattered most to both sides.

Despite the shambolic nature of the afternoon, I didn't hear any of them whinge or grumble. Several Bangor players - and I don't think this was for my benefit - went to their coach, shook hands and said: 'Thanks Ged. Thanks for getting it on.'

I suppose they must have been cheered by the prospect of being back overlooking the Menai Strait by last orders. Their pitch literally overlooks the strait and will no doubt charm the Bolton team when they make their Day Trip to Bangor (Didn't we have a lovely time, the day we went to

Bangor? And so on - Fiddlers Dram, 1980, number three in the UK singles chart) later in the season. It was, supposedly, meant originally to be about a day trip to Rhyl, but that didn't scan, although it is a shorter journey from Bolton.

As for Gerard Keenan, the trip in the opposite direction had been a near-pioneer experience. Only one thing was missing; I watched him like a hawk and at no stage did he autograph anybody's head.

16. Administration:
Not as Dull as it Sounds

Stop fidgeting at the back there. The running of student rugby league is a fascinating story in its own right. Honest. It intertwines in quite an intricate way with the history of the game as a whole, so pay attention. There will be a test at the end.

By a rich co-incidence, at the same time that Ray French was studying English at Leeds - and not playing rugby league - David Oxley was studying English at Oxford - and not playing rugby league. Oxley, from Hull, went up to Worcester College after National Service in 1958 and was destined to play a major role in the game at both academic and national levels.

Although he understandably soft-pedalled this side of things during his time as secretary (later chief executive) of the Rugby Football League, he had rather a distinguished rugby union record at Oxford. He played centre and captained his college, representing the university when some of the top-line players were unavailable, but not playing in the Varsity match nor winning a blue. He was not the only person I spoke to during this research for whom, decades later, this blue business really matters. Given the number of full internationals, including people like Richard Sharp, with whom he was in competition, it hardly counts as a failure.

After taking his teaching qualification, he embarked on a career in private schools. At all four of them, he was involved in coaching union teams, but also got his boys playing league in training. 'It was always a case of them asking if they could,' he claims. 'Perhaps they knew that was the best way of getting out of double English on a Friday afternoon.'

Oxley progressed to the headship of a school in Dover, about as far away from rugby league as you could get, but one morning he spotted a tiny advert in the *Daily Telegraph*. The RFL was seeking a successor to Bill Fallowfield, the Cambridge-educated man at the helm of the League for the previous 28 years. On a whim, he applied. To his surprise, he was short-listed and was the last man interviewed by a formidable panel of six former chairmen of the League.

It was an open secret at the time that the job would go to Bev Risman, former dual-code international and son of the legendary Gus. We last encountered him at Leeds University, we will meet him repeatedly further down the line and he would have been a popular and logical choice. But then the door of the HQ on Chapeltown Road swung open and in walked a public school headmaster from Kent, probably in a roll-neck sweater, with a list of ten things that rugby league needed to change. 'I didn't think I had a chance, so I just went for it.' They gave him the job - and Risman later got the 'consolation prize' of administering the student game - in which role we will meet up with him again shortly. 'I don't think he would have enjoyed the Rugby League job,' Oxley says now. 'He wouldn't have liked the politics.'

Oxley negotiated those politics for the next 18 years, until mandatory retirement at the age of 55 in 1992.

The sheer left-field unlikeliness of his appointment was best pointed up by the circumstances of his first media interview in the role. He was interviewed 'down the line' by Eddie Waring for the BBC after dashing to a studio in London between his performances in the school production of *HMS Pinafore*.

There was fascination at the time at the thought of an Oxford-educated public school head running the working-man's sport, conveniently avoiding the fact that Fallowfield was also an Oxbridge man and in many ways a more patrician figure. One important difference between the two men, however, was in their attitudes to the student game. Fallowfield was widely perceived as lukewarm, reluctant to upset a union establishment within which he had many contacts. 'And I think he was suspicious of an area of the game that might not be under his control,' Oxley says.

He too had his friendships across the great divide - he had been at Oxford with Dudley Wood, for instance - but right from the start he was more enthusiastic than his predecessor about the game in universities and colleges. 'They were disappointed that he had not been more supportive,' he says. 'I hope they found me supportive from day one.'

Oxley was the first man at HQ to fully appreciate the significance of the student sector of the game. Other things needed to be prioritised ahead of it - like healing the rift with BARLA and attracting the sponsorship, at club and national level, to make up the short-fall when it became blindingly obvious that the game could not support itself through gate receipts - but student competition was very much on his 'must do' list. 'I don't think I had anything about the student game in my ten bullet points at the interview - but it was always in my mind.' Not surprisingly, given his background.

The David Oxley/David Howes years at the RFL are generally credited with doing much to adapt the game to changing times. It was also on their watch that student rugby league went global. Oxley followed the 1986 World Cup in New Zealand from a distance. In 1989, it was his responsibility. 'Bob Ashby - bless him - stuck his hand up at the International Board meeting and said "We'll have it!"' The chairman of the Rugby League Council (and of Featherstone Rovers) had effectively volunteered the RFL to host the event.

By the time of that tournament, Martyn Sadler - the Rupert Murdoch of rugby league - was planning his publishing empire. He was succeeded at the head of the student game by... David Oxley, who combined it with being chief executive of the RFL. When he stepped down from that latter role in 1992, one of the candidates to replace him was... Martyn Sadler. (Are you following all this? Because I'm not sure I am.)

'I was invited to apply, but I was never going to get it,' Sadler says. 'Maurice Lindsay wanted it and, in those days, Maurice got what he wanted.'

Oxley, whose last act as chief exec was to present the World Club Challenge trophy to the Brisbane Broncos' captain, Terry Matterson, at Wigan, describes Lindsay as 'positive and supportive' towards student rugby league. He certainly used to glow with satisfaction at having an Oxford classicist and PhD working for him at the RFL. When he was forced into his great leap sideways to head Super League, it was that scholar and former student rugby league activist, Neil Tunnicliffe, who succeeded him.

Oxley and Tunnicliffe were part of an odd little rugby league enclave in the very non-RL town of Harrogate. In fact, Oxley used to be the president of an amateur club there. They used to do rather well against Sunday league teams who assumed, wrongly, that they would be nice, middle-class boys and thus a soft touch. But then the club lost its two stalwarts. 'One committed suicide and one moved to Kazakhstan - where, of course, he could carry on playing rugby league,' he says matter-of-factly. Oxley was one of the great champions of spreading the game to exotic frontiers, by which I mean Kazakhstan, rather than Harrogate.

On the day we meet, in the foyer of a Premier Inn on the outskirts of town that serves as his occasional office, Harrogate is in mourning for the Yorkshire Show, rained off for the first time in living memory. There is something of the pre-industrial Englishman about David Oxley that fits in well with the town. He has never driven, disdains computers and will not have a mobile phone. It is easy to imagine even now, however, how he charmed those sceptical, hard-headed chairmen into giving him the biggest job in the British game.

He can look back with considerable satisfaction on his 18 years in that role. If he wants to look back with unadulterated pleasure, though, he reflects instead on his overlapping period as chairman of the Student Rugby League. 'It was the most enjoyable time I had in rugby league,' he says without hesitation. 'We had our disagreements, but they didn't always have to finish up in a fight outside on the cobbles, with a winner and a loser.'

The number of universities and colleges playing the game went up, he estimates, by an average of six a season during his time in charge. He remains unapologetically partisan over what the student game has contributed to the overall picture. In fact, there are times when he sounds a little like the ultra-patriotic dad in *Goodness Gracious Me*. 'Albert Einstein? Indian! Rudolph Nureyev? Indian!'

The SRL version of this runs something like: 'Brian Carney? He's a product of student rugby league! Jon Wells? He's one of ours!' He played one game, for England against France at Coventry, but you get the general idea. An almost boyish enthusiasm was always one of his prime qualities as an administrator.

David Oxley had a spell as a touchline dad, when his son, Mark, played for Swansea and Welsh Universities. Although he has handed over the SRL chairmanship to John Piercy, a Yorkshireman who made the transition from hooker to referee when he was in the retail business in London, he still keeps a fatherly eye on the student game as a whole. He makes one startling claim, but has three warnings of where it could all go wrong. He believes that the best student teams represent the highest level outside the professional game, anywhere in the world. 'That has been proved when they've played the top BARLA sides in the Challenge Cup. The standard has improved out of sight,' he says.

So, what could possibly go wrong? Well, several things, it appears. The biggest threat to all university sport is the tightening noose of student finance. Faced with the prospect of years in debt, many potential students - and potential sportsmen - are deciding not to bother. The effects of that on falling rolls and course closures is already apparent.

For those who do take the plunge, the pressure is on to make the maximum academic use of their time. That does not necessarily dovetail well with Wednesday afternoons devoted to team sports. Last but not least, there are rumblings of concentrated, two-year degree courses, which would leave precious little slack in the schedule for excelling at rugby league at the same time.

If anything, Bev Risman's relationship with student rugby league is longer and deeper. Son of the great Gus Risman, one of the inaugural members of the RFL's Hall of Fame, he played union for England and league for Leigh, Leeds and Great Britain. He has been an influential figure at all levels of the game, culminating in his recent presidency of the RFL. If he ever gets around to finishing his autobiography, it will be a post-war history of the code.

As you might have noticed, Bev Risman was also involved, almost from the start, in the early days of student rugby league. After several years combining playing with school teaching, he went to Leeds University to take his Masters in the then innovative discipline of Sports Management. He was on the spot, therefore, when Andrew Cudbertson and friends were setting the ball rolling. 'But it never occurred to me what it was going to be the start of,' he admits.

Risman, previously at Bradford Grammar School, got what he wanted from his second degree - a move into further education at Reading University. It was there that he became closely involved with the game in the south, including the student game. 'Trying to change the world,' is the way he puts it. In his next job, at the West London Institute, he launched rugby league and nurtured players like Dave Rotheram and Russ Bridge, who were to have long and varied professional careers. He went after the top job at the RFL because he believed that the game was at a low ebb and needed a change of direction. Although he is far too dignified to say so, you sense that somewhere deep down it still rankles ever so slightly with him.

He was to wield his influence in other ways. He had a year in charge of Fulham, where he tried to put his philosophy for that club into operation. 'I felt then and I feel still that the only way rugby league is ever going to succeed in the south is with southern players,' he says. That was what he filled his team with, including a number of other students alongside Rotheram and Bridge. 'We were competitive, but the club got impatient for immediate results.' Around the same time, the RFL chairman, Bob Ashby, contacted Bev, to ask him to be director of the 1989 Student World Cup. He agreed, provided he had a three-year contract to continue the good work afterwards. As we have seen elsewhere in this story, the tournament was a massive success. 'The sponsors, NatWest, loved it. We got big crowds everywhere and about 3,000 for the final. It also set off a surge of interest in student rugby league and we had dozens of places wanting to set up teams.'

That was not without its problems. 'The attitude of some rugby union people was just ridiculous. They were convinced, quite wrongly, that league would be to the detriment of union. There were a lot of cases of things like notices being ripped down or defaced.'

What advice did he give to fledging rugby league clubs subjected to that sort of low level harassment? 'Not to get into a fight. You achieve nothing by fighting with people. You have to talk to them.'

Risman ran the SRL from his adopted home village of Crowthorne in Berkshire, charging back-and-to between there and the RFL every week. 'I used to hope that at least one referee would cry off every Wednesday, so that I could ref a match,' he says. 'Even though I did it from the half-way line.'

For the 1992 World Cup in Australia, all the arrangements were made with a golfing mate in Crowthorne who happened to be a travel agent. One of the perks of the deal was an unexpected first-class ticket for Bev. 'I would have felt guilty keeping it to myself. Every half hour, I let a different student have it, so he could have a bit of luxury.'

There were 120 players on that flight from the four home nations - probably the biggest rugby league air-lift ever. The occasional upgrade notwithstanding, Risman regards students' adaptability as a key factor in their success as international ambassadors. 'They're so flexible,' he says. 'You can put them anywhere, as long as there's a game at the end of it.' He saw that sort of adaptability not only at World Cups, but also on numerous trips to unlikely places by student teams, culminating in a side that has that as its entire raison d' être, the Student RL Pioneers.

Bev considers himself blessed that, as one door has closed on his career, another has always opened. As he was approaching the RFL's retirement age of 60, it took another turn. 'I thought that something would come up,' he says. 'That something was Super League.' At an age when most people are putting their feet up, he was invited back to the successors to Fulham, the London Broncos. For a while, his two roles overlapped, which produced some interesting contrasts. 'I could go from talking to a young lad who wanted to start a team Exeter University, to sitting across the table from Richard Branson.' Risman had hopes at one stage that the then backer of the Broncos would become the patron saint of the whole game, or, failing that, would prove a natural fit with the students upon whom, as his original market, he built his fortune.

'It would have been great, but he knew how much he wanted to put into rugby league and he stuck to that.

'Anywhere, absolutely anywhere, you go in the country, there are people who want to be involved in rugby league. They've all come through the students. You look at just about any professional club and there are young administrators who have come down that route.'

The same goes for the serried ranks of local development officers - the advance troops in rugby league's continuing campaign for its place in the sun. 'There wouldn't be any of them if it wasn't for the student game,' Risman says.

After a potentially exhausting year as RFL president, his focus has switched to keeping a grandfatherly eye on the progress of 11-year-old Luke Risman, who plays prop for the juniors at the Nottingham Outlaws. 'But he passes like a scrum-half,' he says. Luke is the son of John Risman (Jnr), whom we encountered several chapters ago as the first 'open' double blue for league and union at Oxford. He was on the fringes of the England rugby union squad when a knee ligament injury ended his career in this early 20s.

That brings us to the other John Risman. There is no such thing as an unremarkable Risman, but the man Bev calls brother John, as opposed to son John, has arguably the most compelling story of all to tell.

As a professional with Workington Town, Fulham, Blackpool Borough and Carlisle, he played into his 40s. He played social rugby union until his late 50s. He won league caps for Wales, became and remains the president of the Scottish Rugby League and has been for many years the unofficial development officer for Eastern Europe. One week, he came back from a training camp, somewhere beyond where the Iron Curtain used to hang, to find that his wife had died suddenly. Not surprisingly, he was knocked sideways by that. After a couple of years of drifting, his mates, to try to bring him out of himself, took him on holiday to Majorca. It was there that he met a woman at a party who was looking for a personal trainer. He took the job and the two fell for each other in a big way.

'They just hit it off from the start,' says Bev. 'John would be the first to admit that he's no oil painting, but he scrubs up quite well and he's got a bit of repartee going.' The stranger he charmed turned out to be one Malene Birger, the biggest name in fashion in Denmark. In 2012, they got married and John now divides his time between Danish fashion jaunts and rugby league forays into Eastern Europe. Student rugby league can lead you in some unexpected directions.

Neil Tunnicliffe is further evidence of that. Although he played rugby union at Queen Elizabeth Grammar School in Wakefield, on Sundays it was Trinity. 'Most of the lads at the school played union on a Saturday and watched rugby league on Sunday,' he recalls. He took that affiliation with him to Oxford. 'I was aware that there was rugby league there, but for some reason I never got involved during my first year. The second year, I got myself along there and that was that.'

Tunnicliffe played for Oxford, but missed his chance to appear in the Varsity match with his shoulder injury in 1984. After that, he decided that his true forte was administration and became the president of the university club. It was a John Hobart-style long-term commitment, because he did seven years at Oxford, three years for his Classics degree and another four for his doctorate in Ancient History. At the same time, he began helping Bev Risman, as a volunteer, to run the SRL. When Martyn Sadler stood down as chairman, he was the obvious successor. One of his great sources of satisfaction is that the numbers of student teams went up from 20 to around 60. 'Bev's genius was for getting the basics in place, so that you didn't miss games because teams didn't have a pitch, a kit or opposition. Once you could say to players that there was a match every Wednesday afternoon you had something concrete to offer them.'

Tunnicliffe's first job out in the real world was with the publishers, Kingswood. He and the late Tony Pocock brought out a series of rugby league books that disproved

Fine service: Bev Risman is presented with a caricature on the occasion of his retirement as SRL organiser at Headingley in 1996

the assumption that the reason the game had no literature to speak of was that there was no demand. The insulting implication was that people who were interested in rugby league, by their very nature, didn't read much. Kingswood, until its parent company decided that it was making insufficient profit, showed this up for the class bigotry it was.

Plenty of writers and readers have reason to be grateful for the bridgehead that Kingswood established. Indeed, one of Neil's first tasks was to knock into shape my own first book, *Playing Away* (now only available in very dusty second-hand shops). I am pleased to report that he has made an almost complete recovery.

Tunnicliffe was not an unemployed Latin and Greek-speaking publisher for very long, because he was head-hunted by Maurice Lindsay at the RFL. 'There was no recruitment policy as such,' he says. 'It was just a case of him liking the cut of your jib. He thought someone should give this bright young man a job - so he did.'

What the job exactly consisted off was another question entirely. 'I turned up on a Monday morning and nobody knew who I was or what I was supposed to be doing.' He didn't even have a desk, but worked on a pile of beer crates, kindly donated by the League's sponsors, Stones Bitter.

He could have sat there and just got quietly pissed, but it transpired that his role was really that of a sort of Minister Without Portfolio. If something was not specifically the responsibility of someone else it tended to finish up in the in-tray on top of Tunnicliffe's stack of beer-crates.

Thus it was that he headed the first fact-finding trip to Morocco. 'Basically because nobody else fancied dealing with Hussain M'Barki,' he says. Dr Tunnicliffe was also used extensively when the RFL - and Lindsay in particular - wanted to convey the message that the old class barriers were a thing of the past. 'I was wheeled out for certain meetings,' he says, 'a bit like an exhibit in a museum.' Somewhere along the line, he acquired the title of deputy chief executive. 'Because they didn't know what else to call me.' It was a title with consequences; nobody cares very much who is Vice-President of the United States until someone shoots the President and then it suddenly becomes very important indeed. The equivalent of the lone sniper in Dallas was Lindsay's resignation to take the helm at Super League (Europe) ' just as those who wanted him out of the RFL were closing in. Tunnicliffe, as deputy, took over the biggest job in the game, initially on an interim basis and later confirmed in the post. No amount of study of the Medes and Persians or the City-State of Origin fixtures between Athens and Sparta could have prepared him for the battlefield of warring factions he had inherited.

'In effect, there were four governing bodies, all deeply mistrustful of each other. I don't think I was prepared for the internal politics,' he says. There were over 20 cases of litigation pending, most of them from member clubs, but also including the big one from the ARL, who wanted their share of the profit declared from the 1995 World Cup, but which no-one seemed able to actually locate. For Tunnicliffe, the legal and political strands became entangled with the personal, a woman scorned and a messy resignation. 'It was very regrettable,' he says. 'But I'd been trying to get out for months.'

Appropriately, our conversation about all this took place in the bar of the Queen's Hotel in Leeds, where Eddie Waring used to hold court. Less relevantly, it was where the then much-admired Great British eccentric, Jimmy Savile, had lain in state the previous year. Reputation, as the Roman emperors knew, can be a fragile thing.

Tunnicliffe did what any unemployed classical scholar would do; he became a consultant. More than ever during our latest recession, consultancy has looked suspiciously like the only growth industry in Britain. 'I decided I'd give it six months and, if my phone wasn't ringing, I'd have to go and get a proper job.' He needn't have worried; he has been in steady demand ever since, notably by two sports preparing themselves for the London Olympics - wrestling and volleyball. Wrestling particularly reminds him of rugby league, he says, not because of all the nonsense that goes on after the tackle, but because it is equally prone to splits and internecine strife.

With commendable honesty, he also admits to 'doing quite a bit of work on the Dark Side.' Along with another league export, Joe Lydon, he is currently working on establishing a Great Britain Sevens squad. It seems a shame that someone so imbued with rugby league, at student level and beyond, should have taken that turning. Bright young man; someone should offer him a proper job.

Niel Wood has had a succession of proper jobs in rugby league. Even in his home-town of Hull, however, his early exposure to the code was limited. He remembers playing in a Sevens at primary school in a deluge and Johnny Whiteley turning up as promised in his wellies to hand out the trophies. Although he played league in the street, his secondary school was exclusively devoted to football - a game at which he excelled. When he went to Liverpool University to read Economics, however, he found himself pining for rugby league.

After some early success, the university club was virtually in hibernation. It took two years to revive it and their first game against Hull saw them beaten 82-0. From that inauspicious start, Liverpool built rapidly and, in his post-graduate year, they were the champions - the first of five consecutive titles. 'We just got a critical mass of good players,' he says, citing in particular the former Warrington winger, Paul Wharton. Wood had left by the time Liverpool reached the final of the John Player Amateur Sevens in 1981, but remembers the stir they caused - union players with assumed names and all.

The remarkable thing about it is that, all this time, Wood was playing semi-pro soccer for teams like South Liverpool, Southport and Scarborough as a tenacious midfielder, including one memorable encounter with a recuperating Kenny Dalglish. 'I hated it,' he says. 'Hated the attitudes and the morality. The only thing I didn't hate was the brown envelope at the end of the week.' He also makes the startling claim that there are people at this level of football who are madder than anyone he has ever met in rugby league. When you think of some of the people he has had to deal with, that is a truly remarkable assertion.

His other problem was that he was still missing rugby league too much. On his teaching practice, he succeeded in introducing it to a school in Anfield literally in the shadow of the Kop. He was still playing for Liverpool Uni and some of his fifth formers were so keen on the game that they went on the bus for an away game at Hull, where Mr Wood promptly lost them. His first permanent job - lucky to get one, under the circumstances - was at the union-playing Rainford High School, where he organised league training session in the dinner-hour for pupils including Dave Rotheram, who went on to have a significant career as a player and a coach.

Niel made the decision to junk his football career in favour of unpaid rugby league. He went to Pilkington's in St Helens and was player of the year in the inaugural season of the National Conference League. 'It was a great experience,' he says now. 'A great feeling across all the clubs of being involved together in something exciting.' He found that he came in handy in unexpected ways. One night he arrived at training and found one of Pilks' forwards waiting for him. He needed a translation of the referee's rather florid report on his sending off, because he wasn't sure what 'recalcitrant' meant.

Wood had found the thing he was meant to do and that thing was evangelising on behalf of rugby league. He spent the best part of a decade in development roles in Oldham and Rochdale and worked alongside the late Peter Deakin on another boundary-pushing venture - BUSCARLA, the British Upper Schools and Colleges Amateur Rugby League Association. His first administrative involvement with students was through the Ireland team, with which he had an affinity through his wife's family. He got his dream job, running the SRL, when Bev Risman stepped aside and he was recognised as the obvious candidate to replace him.

The SRL he was running was by this stage a limited company under the umbrella of the RFL, from which it received a £75,000 annual grant. 'I was so careful with it that I hardly spent any of the first year's money,' he says. 'After that, we always generated at least twice as much as our grant ourselves.' That income, from sponsorship, outside grants and the rest, enabled the SRL to build up its representative structure and its touring calendar. Nobody has organised and travelled on more of these trips than Wood himself, each with its own stock of memories and stories. He was, for instance, with the kilted and bagpipe-playing Scots on a tour to Venice and Belgrade. Finding the streets of the former city flooded, he and John Risman (Snr) tried to negotiate advantageous rates for a gondola ride for the whole party. They were getting nowhere until it transpired that one of the gondoliers was from Aberdeen.

Perhaps with that in mind, he would dearly love to see a regular competition in Scoland, to go along with the embryonic one in Ireland that took its first, faltering steps in 2012. He now wears a number of hats at the RFL, some of them with big feathers attached. He is director of European development as well as acting head of communications, with the unenviable task of trying to reverse the decline in coverage of the game in national newspapers, but the ties that still bind him to the student game remain strong. It is, he is convinced, despite the ever-tightening purse-strings, capable of a good deal of future expansion. 'We've hardly scratched the surface yet,' he says.

One final thought from him on what we might call playing the long game. Where does he stand on the identity of the most significant player to come through student rugby league?

'I could say it was Andy Raleigh,' he muses. 'Or I could say it was someone who was pretty crap, but signed a big sponsorship cheque.'

For the first decade of the 21st century, the SRL's king-pin was yet another member of what might be termed the Hull Mafia. Matt Jeffery got the bug early, at a primary school on Ings Road that fielded, he says, the smallest and scruffiest rugby league team in the city, but beat everyone. After secondary school, he did not go straight to university but worked for three years on the docks, playing for Hull Dockers and for Hull KR's Academy team. By the time he enrolled on a three-year teaching course at Liverpool John Moores, he was pretty much a man among boys.

"I had no idea there was such a thing as student rugby league and, when I found that there was, I thought it would be just a case of 80 minutes and into the pub.' At John Moores - named after its benefactor, the founder of the Littlewood's Pools empire - it was taken a little more seriously than that. There were players of professional quality like Paul Topping and Graeme Close on board and Jeffery fitted straight into the side that topped the table and won the knock-out Cup by beating UWIC in his first year there, 1998-9.

'I was that bit older, that bit more physically mature, and it made a difference,' he says. He played his way up the representative ladder, captaining the national side and, after graduation, he was invited to apply for the role of manager of the SRL. It was a job that he did for nine years and in which he is able to point to a number of solid achievements, including raising the profile of the Varsity game through television coverage and finally winning a three-Test series against Australia in 2011. He can also claim a slow but steady consolidation of the numbers of universities and colleges playing the game, although it sometimes looks like one step forward, one step back as the weaker teams come and go.

Jeffery does not agonise over trying to achieve saturation coverage. 'You could say that it has reached a plateau, but we got the game played in the places that matter, with standards at the top end going up all the time,' he says.

And yet Matt Jeffery's story is evidence that everything is not always sunlight and harmony in the world of student rugby league, No sooner was that landmark victory achieved over the Australians than he was out of work. From a position of relative autonomy, the SRL was absorbed into the Rugby League's Community Game department, bracketed with BARLA, the Armed Services and the schools. That meant redundancies among administrators and Jeffery was the unlucky man. It is an experience that still rankles with him. 'It was bitter,' he admits. 'And I don't think they've found a way of doing the job better, just a way of doing it cheaper.' He was supply teaching when I tracked him down, but is due to take up a post at a college in East Yorkshire.

He no longer has any involvement with rugby league. 'After 14 years of your life revolving around it, that's quite a wrench,' he says.

Under the new structure, the buck now stops with the RFL's education services manager, Kate Hebden. Her responsibilities encompass the schools, the colleges and the universities and she has no doubt that it is the middle stratum - sixth forms that were - which she needs to bring up to speed and make more genuinely national. If that is one aim for the future, then regular competition in Scotland is another. Perhaps even closer to her heart is the target of a full-time women's league. 'The interest is there, but, unfortunately, if there is nothing on the ground, they finish up playing rugby union,' Kate says.

■ As promised, an exam question to check whether you've been concentrating:

Using diagrams, trace the career trajectories of a) Bev Risman b) David Oxley c) Neil Tunnicliffe, with particular attention to their points of intersection.

17. Women's Studies:
Mrs Pankhurst's Legacy

Given the subject matter, it's only appropriate that at least part of this book should be an education to the writer as well as the reader. In no facet of the game is that more true for me than in women's rugby league. I've seen a few matches over the years and enjoyed them, but they have usually felt like add-ons to a male competition. One exception was back in 1997, when I saw an absolute stormer between the New Zealand Maori and Samoa as part of the Polynesian Festival at Carlaw Park in Auckland. I had the onerous task of picking the Person of the Match on that occasion - a bit of a minefield when you don't really want to upset any of them.

New Zealand have been the dominant force in Women Students' RL. The game in this country is rather puny by comparison, with the girls held back by some of the same problems that their male counterparts had to tackle decades ago. 'The problem has been that female rugby league is not on the BUCS accredited list and therefore is not funded,' says the chair of the RFL's Female Steering Group and vice-chair of the SRL, Pat Crawshaw. 'It's Catch 22 - the teams can't attract players because it is not on the list and they can't get on the list because there aren't enough players or teams for it to be acknowledged.'

Julia Lee, perhaps the most high-profile woman in the game after Kath Hetherington, thanks to her pioneering work as a referee, has tried to get to grips with this dilemma, but, at the moment, there is precious little competition between colleges and universities.

'It's a bit frustrating really,' says Julia, who was briefly the stuff of headlines when she refereed her Varsity match in 1998. 'There was a lot of coverage at the time. It put the game on the map by having a woman referee. I didn't feel used, though, because I knew what I was letting myself in for.'

There is no saying how far she would have gone in refereeing, had it not been for a serious back injury. Instead, she has opted for working in development roles at the RFL, including a particular concentration on the women's game.

'At one time, we had eight or ten student teams, but it's going to be hard to get it back to that again,' she says. The problem, as so often, is funding. The game as a whole is getting less from Sport England and the figures it needs to show to get more are for participation among males from their teens to 20s. Getting a female student competition up and running seems a distant prospect in the current climate.

When there was one, it was dominated to a surprising degree by an unexpected name - the University of Luton (now part of the University of Bedfordshire.) 'And there was nothing butch about them,' I am assured by an unreconstructed member of the RFL staff. 'If you saw them on a night out, you wouldn't think "rugby team".'

In the interests of balance, I have to acknowledge the

experience of my middle daughter's school friend - a rugby league fanatic - who went to training when she arrived at her new university. She was back a couple of hours later, complaining that they were all shaven-haired toughies and had beaten her up.

It is on the representative scene that things have been happening. There is an annual match against a French side from Aquitaine and this year, for the first time, the Women Students faced a Women Teachers' XIII in what is intended to become a yearly event. John Piercy attended that inaugural fixture in his capacity as SRL chairman and came away greatly impressed by the standard. 'They played like it really meant everything to them,' he said.

The jewel in the crown, however, is the Pankhurst Cup. Since 2008, the students have played an annual fixture against the Combined Services. The name of the trophy is an inspired evocation of the themes of exclusion and enfranchisement that run through so much of modern history - and through all of rugby league.

Emmeline (Emily) Pankhurst was born in 1858 in the Moss Side district of Manchester, but lived for part of her life in Seedley. The site of that home is just a hefty kick from The Willows; or maybe, given her propensity for direct action, just a well-thrown brick away.

Mrs Pankhurst was the leader of the Suffragette movement and certainly, a century later, its best-remembered name. Even Emily Davison, who died after throwing herself in front of the King's horse, is, by comparison, forgotten. The Suffragettes were a fractious lot, prone to falling out among themselves, but that is not where their affinity with rugby league ends. There is a splendid irony in two of the institutions that have been most historically resistant to sexual equality - universities and the armed forces - playing each other at a game that was also once excluded.

The students pick their squad after a couple of open trials, under the eagle eye of their coach, Mark Brennan. His previous experience, apart from coaching both sexes at Cronton College, was training Widnes' scholarship lads. 'Even if the sheer power is less in the women's game, the passion and the commitment is exactly the same,' he says.

The students warmed up in 2012 by beating a Women Teachers' team in the first of what is scheduled to be an annual series. They still haven't won the Pankhurst Cup, but they are getting closer every year. Last time, they went down 18-8 at RAF Cranwell in Lincolnshire. The game ended early because of an injury to one of the students. At least they got further than a women's match between Bradford and Whinmoor a couple of weeks later - not strictly a student game, but one in which a number of students played. That was abandoned after eight minutes because of a broken leg and a broken collar-bone. It was a reminder of one thing it shares with any other variety of full-contact rugby league; you can get hurt.

It is also worth noting the strong female role in running the student game as a whole. As the head of education services at the RFL, the buck now stops with Kate Hebden, whilst Tracey O'Mara, based in Warrington, keeps it on track on a match-by-match basis. They are the women without whom the men's game wouldn't happen.

18. Metallurgy:
Gloucestershire Gold and Other Experiments

When the Rugby Football league announced its controversial plans to expand the third tier of the professional game, Championship 1, by admitting three clubs from new areas, it initially selected three operations built on models quite distinct from each other.

On the one hand, there is what might be called the Fulham template of starting a club from scratch on a football ground, with the landlord and parent club often labouring under the illusion that there was money to be made from the arrangement. Other notable examples of this have been Carlisle, Cardiff, Kent and Southend Invicta and, via a circuitous route, North Wales Crusaders at Wrexham.

I would love to be able to give you instances of stability and long-term success being achieved in this way, but there are none.

On the other hand, it is theoretically possible for a grassroots club to start on a park pitch, to be run from the back room of a pub and to gradually build its strength to the point where it can make the transition to the semi-pro game. There are plenty that have had that vision, but precious few who have made it. You can't count South Wales or Gateshead, which are both essentially the stubborn residue of previous failures; London Skolars have a better claim. Hemel Hempstead, who will follow in their footsteps in 2013, could put down a bigger marker for British expansion ambitions, even if it has taken them 30 years since they were founded by the Australian, Bob Brown, who is still their driving force, to get where they are today.

Hemel are typical of nothing, but then neither are the third members of this triumvirate - the University of Gloucestershire All-Golds. This is where the real ground-breaking stuff is going on.

Cheltenham, where they are based, might be more readily associated with National Hunt racing, the Ladies' College and the Literary Festival, but it has its own little niche in rugby league history. It was there, on 15 February 1908, that rugby league's first Test series was decided. The opponents for the Northern Union, as it was then, had come literally from the ends of the earth - the New Zealand All-Golds, so called to distinguish them from the All-Blacks. It was meant to be a term of disparagement, but has become a badge of honour. The pioneering venture ended in success on the field and tragedy off it and it is all the more iconic for that. The success was sealed by an 8-5 win at Cheltenham that gave the Kiwis a 2-1 series victory, with a side that included the legendary name of Lance Todd. The tragedy came on the way home when Albert Henry Baskiville (or Baskerville, the spelling varies), the Wellington postal clerk who had initiated the tour, died of influenza in Sydney.

The question remains: Why Cheltenham, of all places?

Because expansion is not a new preoccupation in rugby league. More than 100 years ago, they were already trying to push back the boundaries and the West Country was seen as potentially fertile ground. A century later, Lionel Hurst came to very much the same conclusion. You remember Lionel; we met him and his personal vortex of restless energy in Sheffield and in Oxford. Now running his criminal law practice in Cheltenham, the league connections of that area continue to resonate with him. There were three Gloucestershire men in the Rorke's Drift Test. Man of the match in that Cheltenham Test - which happens to fall on Lionel's birthday - was not the debutant Billy Batten, but Billy Holder from Gloucester. Just recently, he has run into his grandson, plus the grandson of Alf Wood, another celebrated player of that era. There is a plaque marking the site - now built upon - of the 1908 game. Rugby league and the story of the original All-Golds has featured in the Literary Festival. Their modern successors will have Baskerville's signature - or Baskiville's - sewn into their playing shirts.

The most lasting memorial to the rugby league men of Gloucestershire, however, would be a successful club run along the unique lines Hurst has in mind. Unique? Well, he admits to some inspiration from Hartpury College, four miles north of Gloucester, a rugby union hot-house which attracts and develops talent. The difference is that the University of Gloucester's top rugby league side will be competing in a professional division, the epicentre of which is 200 miles away - probably somewhere between Oldham and Rochdale, both of whom find themselves marooned in it. 'It's the most fantastic sporting story of all time,' says Lionel. 'I don't believe in under-selling it. If it works, it's the future of rugby league.'

So, what does the future look like? Before entry into

Championship 1, UniGlos are running five teams - the All-Golds and the All-Blues in the student game and Academy sides at under 14, under 16 and under 18. From 2013, they will also have their semi-pro team, facing the likes of the Roughyeds and the Hornets. There were two significant autumn announcements - the appointment of the former Kiwi international, Brad Hepi, as head coach and the first signing of a professional player. Richard Jones had been playing at Keighley and the unveiling of him as the first new All-Gold was timed for Bonfire Night, which happened to be the date of the original All-Golds' match against that Yorkshire club. Rugby league is sometimes accused of forgetting its own history; not Lionel Hurst, he remembers the tiniest details.

Jones, a strapping forward who made 12 appearances in 2012, has been persuaded to take his MA at the University of Gloucester and there will be more signings of that sort. 'But what we don't want to do,' says Hurst, 'is to import a whole team from the North of England.' There are 26 players this academic year who are there on rugby league scholarships and the flow of talent, he firmly believes, will one day be in the opposite direction. 'We are going to produce a whole lot of players who are going to play Super League and play for England,' Hurst says. 'We can do that, because we are going to approach it professionally.'

There are some specific advantages for a professional club based on a university campus. A crop of muscle strains? Shout down the academic pit-shaft for half a dozen physiotherapy students. A publicity push needed? Send for the trainee journalists. In theory, university and rugby club become each other's raw material.

It's a fascinating experiment, which may or may not work. The frailty of one of the alternative blueprints, however, was all too obvious when Northampton failed to make the starting line, pulling out months before they were due to enter Championship 1. They set some sort of record for the sport by folding before they had played a single game. That left the Rugby Football League in need of a replacement. Coventry, a club with long-nurtured roots and strong student connections, not least through their head of rugby, the former student international prop, Alan Robinson, who was once sent off within 90 seconds of the start of a Test against France, were not quite ready and are 'on a promise' for 2014. The ones to put their hands up were Oxford - and, although, they will not be a student team as such, the links look like being pretty strong. For one thing, they will play their home games at the university's sports complex at Iffley Road. It should prove an evocative location, particularly the running track where Roger Bannister ran the first four-minute mile on May 6 1954. That, incidentally, was the day after the 102,000 crowd at Odsal for the Warrington-Halifax Challenge Cup final replay. I can't help wondering whether anyone was at both events. Throw in Hungary's 7-1 victory over England a couple of weeks later and it was quite a month for sport, but I digress.....

Although not composed exclusively of students, the Oxford club will represent a line of continuity through Oxford University and Hurst's previous brain-child, the Oxford Cavaliers. At their first open trial, Oxford Brookes University was particularly well represented. There are echoes from other corners of the rugby league world, in the involvement of Tony Colquitt, a successful chief executive in his time at St Helens, and Simon Lee, the Dr Frankenstein who flicked the switch to create the monster that was Leeds Met. It should be interesting.

As so often with ideas that seem to have sprung from nowhere, there are intriguing historic parallels, if not necessarily direct ones. Back in 2000, there was briefly a student team at the bottom of the Northern Ford Premiership, masquerading under the name of the Lancashire Lynx.

How the Lynx came to be in Lancashire - at Chorley's ironically misnamed Victory Park, to be precise - is a long and convoluted story in itself. It begins with Blackpool Borough, continues with Springfield Borough, Trafford Borough and Chorley Borough and features a couple of diversions back to the seaside with Blackpool Gladiators and finally, we think, Blackpool Panthers, who won the club's first trophy in almost 60 years, the British Coal 9s, and promptly imploded. Somewhere in the middle of that lot are the Lancashire Lynx, who played at various times at Preston North End and Preston Grasshoppers, but who in the year 2000 were at Chorley - but not to be confused, of course, with Chorley Lynx. The previous season they had appointed Steve Hampson, the former Wigan and Great Britain full-back and fitness guru to, among others, Andrew Flintoff and Lee Westwood, as coach. He succeeded an equally illustrious name from the game's recent history, the New Zealand forward, Kevin Tamati. Despite this periodic sprinkling with stardust, they remained the epitome of a struggling club, although they did reach the final of the Anglo-French Treize Tournoi in 1998. Midway through the 2000 season, North End, who had continued to prop up the Lynx even though they no longer played at Deepdale, nor indeed in Preston, let it be known that they were no longer going to do so. Enter, stage left, the cavalry on their white horses, otherwise known as the Student Rugby League.

Niel Wood and the GB Students' coach, Vinny Webb, sat down with the Lynx chairman and local baker, Henry Morris, to discuss an imaginative rescue plan. The SRL would take over the running of the club and they would import the cream of student talent to play for it. Over the best pies in the Rugby League - official - they agreed the deal in principle.

Webb would join Hampson as his assistant, but then the former Test star resigned, leaving Webb holding the baby. His previous entanglement with the many-faced Boroughs, Lynxes etcetera had been as a loan player at Trafford when he was on Rochdale Hornets' books, but now he was approaching it from a different angle. He started to bring in the students, but meanwhile another faction on the board had invited the former Great Britain, Wigan and Leeds coach, Maurice Bamford, to take the reins. Bamford coached more clubs than anyone in the history of the game; one of the titles he earned was The First Aid Man, for his work with apparent basket cases. He aimed to take the club in a different direction altogether and a bunch of students was not part of his road-map. 'He turfed everyone out,' recalls Webb. For one game at Keighley, the team selected in Chorley travelled across the Pennines, only to find another set of Yorkshire-based players in the away dressing room getting changed.

'It was an interesting time,' Vinny says, with some understatement. Whoever was in charge and however you divide up the responsibility, it was quite a season. The Lynx won just one game, under Hampson and against Whitehaven, and used a mind-boggling total of 72 players. There are some interesting names among them, both student and non-student. Alan Robinson is one from the first category; the second includes Jason Demetriou and two members of the Farrell clan, Phil and Mick.

It was a short-lived experiment. By the 2001 season, Bamford was replaced by another big name, Graeme West, the club was now known as Chorley Lynx and was run on more conventional lines - or as conventional as it got. They finished next to bottom.

Could it have worked? Webb is certain that it could. 'The top end of the student game was already run more professionally than the bottom end of the NFP,' he argues and he is well qualified to judge. The leading forward in the amateur game, he had a couple of seasons with Rochdale (and Trafford) before deciding that it wasn't for him and going back to player-coach Woolston. From there, he applied for and got the GB Students' coaching job in 1997.

'The idea at Chorley was that we should prepare our best players for the World Cup, but it would help the club as well. We were ahead of our time and it's interesting too see what has happened since, at the London Skolars and now the University of Gloucestershire.'

Mention of the London Skolars steers us in the direction of another way in which student rugby league can interact with the game as a whole. As far back as the late-60s, the SRL aspired to having a club to which graduates who had developed a taste for the game could gravitate. Leeds Academicals followed a similar logic, as did Mancunians, set up by Stefan Hopewell, another Trojan in these areas of activity. The difference was that the Skolars became a semi-professional club in the Rugby League itself. In both cases, it was a bid to get to grips with the issue of transition - a big theme in development work. It's all very well introducing people to rugby league in higher education, the argument goes, but where do they go afterwards? The Skolars are a mis-spelt attempt to answer that question, at least for the London area; mis-spelt, by the way, because of a sponsorship deal with Skol lager 'that almost came off.' They money never arrived, but the name did and it stuck. The other issue of nomenclature at the Skolars is that their driving force, the memorably named Hector McNeil, is not really called Hector. He was, rather mundanely, christened Ian, but has always preferred his second name, which has echoes of Hector McNeil, the Secretary of State for Scotland in Clement Atlee's governments. Do not, on any account, become confused by the presence of a Hector McNeill (with two Ls) on each side in the American War of Independence. Yes, I know I make it seem straightforward, but it took me days to sort out that lot.

The fact remains that there are advantages to being called Hector. 'It's quite useful in sport,' he says. 'If someone shouts "Hector" you've a good idea it's for you, because there aren't many more. It also toughens you up a bit, because people are always taking the piss out of you.'

That, Hector, is what we call Boy Named Sue Syndrome and, as you say, the wrestler, Shirley Crabtree, uncle of Eorl, is another well-known victim.

Hector first had the micky taken out of him on the rugby pitch for clubs like Stockton, Middlesbrough and West Hartlepool. He was a hooker and, as he says, 'rugby union through and through.' That remained the case even when he went to university at Hull, where he played two seasons of union before having a nibble at league in his final year. 'I just loved it,' he says. 'I'd always wanted the ball in my hands and as a hooker in league you've got it all the time.' If there is one position in the two codes that represents a 100 per cent contrast in that respect, hooker it must be.

Hull had a strong league side at this stage, thanks largely to a healthy intake of talent and experience from across the Pennines, and Hector was at least half-way to having the 13-a-side bug. When he went to work as a trader in the Stock Exchange, he played both codes, as and when it suited him, but league took over when he went to Warwick for his Master of Business Administration degree.

'I was only 24 and they don't usually take people as young as that, but having worked in the Stock Exchange probably swung it.' His arrival at Warwick was timely, because the university, which had previously only played league as a joint venture with nearby Coventry, was in the process of launching a stand-alone club. He went along to the first training session, convened by Bev Risman, and ended up coaching and running the team. 'It suited me, because I'd always wanted to be involved in administration as well as playing, but it was quite a challenge getting it going. We had a great season; we took quite a few scalps and even went to Ireland and played the Dublin Blues.' That year, there was a two-tier set-up for students at Warwick. You could play on Wednesdays for your university and at weekends for a composite side called Coventry Students. McNeil, needless to say by this stage, did both.

On his return to London, he needed a side to play for and among those at which he lobbed up were Hemel Hempstead and Hornsey Lams. Not Lambs, please note, as in lambs to the slaughter, although there were a few of those, but Lams, as in the Malaysian restaurant that sponsored them. Very tasty satay after their games, I recall. As he tried to find a congenial club, Hector became aware that there were other graduates rattling around the capital with the game problem. 'At least half of student players were new to the game and 30 per cent of graduates gravitate to London. That adds up to a lot of potential players, so we decided that what we needed was a club of our own.' Thus it was that, in 1995, the Student Rugby League Old Boys came into existence, as the welding together of two completely different ideas. Old boys' rugby union was a well-developed concept in London, but nobody had thought of applying it to rugby league. Despite the new club's name, it was never exclusively for ex-students nor for rugby league players, in the same way that it is usually no barrier to old boys' rugby union if you happen not to have gone to that particular school. 'We were about 60/40,' says Hector, meaning 60 per cent former students, still probably a uniquely high proportion.

Initially, they played in the London League, with a home pitch on Hackney Marshes. In 1997, under the name of the

North London Skolars, they joined the Southern Conference League. Discussions had been well advanced with Skol lager over naming rights, but when the deal fell through they lost the sponsor but kept the name. There was something about the in-joke that the country's most highly educated team couldn't spell that made it irresistible. The Skolars moved to the New River Stadium, at the opposite end of White Hart Lane from Spurs, and became plain old London Skolars. They graduated to the National Conference League and in 2002 became the first club since Featherstone Rovers in 1921 to make the transition from amateur club to professional when they were elevated into what was then National League 2. There, in the third tier of the pro game, they have been ever since, usually struggling, but in 2012 within sight of a play-off place. If that remains an aspiration for the future, we are entitled to ask what the Skolars have achieved so far. They have shown that it is possible to run a club that is largely unsuccessful (in playing terms) very cheaply. They have also been a little font of innovation, staging the annual Capital Challenge against the London Broncos at the Honorable Artillery Company's ground amid the skyscrapers of the City. It earns the Skolars more than all their home fixtures in Championship 1.

It is also a magnet for a 'city boy' audience, some but not all of whom have had some exposure to rugby league as students. 'We couldn't get them to New River, but we can get them there,' Hector says. 'There were three rugby league matches listed in the *Daily Telegraph*'s sports calendar for this year [2013] and the Capital Challenge was one of them.'

Then there is Friday Night Lights - a Skolars home game the evening before the Challenge Cup final and another gathering point for league people. The New River Stadium has also hosted the Middlesex 9s, as well as occasional beer festivals at the back of the stand - and they don't half make semi-pro rugby league look a whole lot better.

Most of all, you have to ask the question that, if the Skolars weren't doing it, who would be playing at that level, somewhere between Hackney Marshes and Super League, in London? The answer is nobody; and it is only the structure that the old student ethos gave it, even though only 15 per cent or so of their players are graduates now - including John Paxton, who gave that famous Ashes clinching pass to Jimmy Keinhorst and made more appearances than anyone for the Skolars in 2012 - that has made it sustainable. 'There's nothing organic about it,' admits Hector. 'It was a case of making it happen.'

It may or may not surprise you that McNeil does not throw an unconditional welcome mat in front of the three new clubs who are trying, in their various ways, to follow in their footsteps. In the case of Hemel Stags, the reservations he expresses are very much old-school rugby league. 'They have the best chance, because they've been around for 30 years, but they're too close to us. They're only a 15 minute drive away; that's not expansion into new areas. We'll be competing for the same players and there's not enough around as it is. It's already causing wage inflation. It's bad enough with rugby union. They are offering young players £15,000 contracts and it's a big attraction.'

Oxford's prospects he dismisses by saying 'there's nothing there,' whilst he warns Gloucester that if they think their students will be good enough for Championship 1, they are in for a severe shock. 'It's taken us nine years to get as competitive as we are now,' he says. 'I don't think they know what they've got themselves into.'

To which Gloucester, Oxford and Hemel Hempstead may reply that they will just have to prove everybody wrong, a little like the London Skolars have done by their very survival.

19. First Class Honours:
Raleigh Round the Standard

In the course of writing this book, I have not infrequently had to ask people a difficult but inevitable question.

Of all the thousands who have played rugby league as students, who has been the most notable and successful as a professional? Who has graduated with the highest Honours? One name has cropped up time and time again - Andy Raleigh. He was born in Huddersfield, with two PE teachers for parents, and played as a boy for various junior sides in the area. When he went off to the University of Newcastle to read Geography in 1999, he was only vaguely aware that there might be rugby league there. 'But I went to the freshers' fair and they had a stall there,' he says. 'I went to the first training session and I was involved from then on.'

Rugby league started at Newcastle Uni in 1994; before that, students who fancied a game had to try their luck at the rival University of Northumbria, previously - and still to some - Newcastle Polytechnic. We've noticed before that the mutual animosity between long-established universities and pumped-up polytechnics can be strong. It is certainly a factor in the tension, on and off the rugby field, between Leeds and Leeds Met. If some of the websites I've been browsing are any guide, the relationship between the two in Newcastle is particularly toxic. Newcastle University students routinely refer to Northumbria as 'the Poly' and Northumbrians adopt that as a badge of pride to distinguish themselves from the supposed snobs and elitists down the street, who are apparently the sort of wimps who would wear jackets and scarves on a night out in the Bigg Market. A lot of the heat generated by the student press on Tyneside recently concerned which rugby union club had the more disgusting initiation ceremonies. Thankfully, eating dog-food seems to be less of a pre-requisite for signing up with either rugby league club.

Inverting the usual relationship, it is the former poly which can claim the rugby league seniority in Newcastle. In '94, it was a Yorkshireman, Jim Sephton, who set up a club at the uni, with the help of the RFL's development officer, Mick Hogan. It was five years before they really took off, coinciding with an intake that included Raleigh and a number of other experienced players from the rugby league heartlands. 'There were a few lads from Wigan and Leigh, as well as from Yorkshire,' he says. 'We had a pretty handy team and we stuck together all through.' Rob Powell, later to coach the London Broncos, was just making the transition from playing to coaching, because of injury, and Newcastle won a couple of trophies. They also won a play-off match in unique fashion when, after multiple postponements for foul weather, victory over Bradford was decided by a game of Paper, Scissors and Stone.

If they were a pretty useful side, then it was Raleigh who

stood out. By the end of his first year, he had played for the North East and for England, including the famous tournament in Kazan. He also toured Australia and New Zealand with Great Britain. 'There were some fantastic opportunities,' he says. In his final year, there were opportunities for professional clubs to run the rule over him.

'Mark Aston came to watch us play the Police and he offered me a part-time contract to play for Sheffield Eagles. Unlike most clubs, they always had their eye on the student game. They also signed Jack Howieson, who I'd played against for England against Scotland, and he's still there.'

Co-incidentally, we were discussing all this on the day that Aston was awarded an honorary degree by Sheffield Hallam University. Thanks to him, the links between the Eagles and the university are strong indeed.

In 2012, they had two Hallam graduates - Howieson and Pat Smith - in their first-team squad and in the 2013 academic year there were scheduled to be eight signed players doing courses there. 'We've got the scholarships and the player pathways in place and my dream is to give youngsters the opportunity to play full-time professional rugby league for the Sheffield Eagles whilst getting an education,' Aston said. He has since moved closer to that aspiration by announcing the formation of a new club, the Sheffield Hallam Eagles, to play in the National Conference South from 2013.

The original Eagles certainly proved to be a good launch-pad for Raleigh. After two years with them, he was signed by Hull Kingston Rovers, just gathering momentum for their successful push for promotion. He beat them into Super League by signing for the Huddersfield Giants, playing for them against St Helens in the 2006 Challenge Cup final. In five years there, he earned the reputation as one of the most reliable forwards in the game - not flashy, but very, very sound. He is now with Wakefield, shining in the surprise run to the play-offs in 2012, and playing under the coaching of Richard Agar, who was the England Students' coach for that trip to Kazan. Apparently, his team-mates refer to Raleigh as 'The Brains Trust'. I don't know whether that's better or worse than the way that Liverpool's footballers used to call Steve Heighway and Brian Hall - graduates both - 'Big Bamber' and 'Little Bamber', after Bamber Gascoigne, the question-master on - what else? - *University Challenge.*

It has been a good career and it's not over yet. It has involved a certain amount of juggling of commitments, but Raleigh is happy with the path he chose. He owes the student game much - friends for life as well as his start as a professional. He is also evidence for Vinny Webb's contention that clubs should look a little harder for players who could make the same sort of transition. 'There are some gems out there,' he says. Rugby league also did Raleigh's academic career no harm. There is a persistent rumour that he got a first - notoriously difficult for a university sportsman. He didn't; he got a good 2:1, as opposed to the more typical, middle-of-the-road 2:2 (or a Desmond, as it is popularly known). He plans one day to put that degree to work in the field of player welfare. If that is one for the future, after his playing days are over, then he also keeps an eye on the team where it all started, turning to, or clicking first on Newcastle University's results.

To seek them out, he has to look in the National North division - the second tier of the SRL pyramid - because it is Northumbria who carry the Geordie banner in the elite National Premier or Super Six. Neither they nor any one else, however, has produced a professional player of quite the durability and effectiveness of Andy Raleigh. Mentions in dispatches, though, to his contemporary as a student and at Huddersfield, Paul Smith, to Brian Carney, for sheer dramatic impact, and to Ady Spencer, a talented player at Super League level, as well as cause célèbre at Cambridge. Andy Proctor was another who made the transition to being a good pro, signing for Wakefield after playing for Liverpool John Moores and Saddleworth Rangers. He is now a senior lecturer at UCLAN in Preston. There should be many more candidates to follow, not least the Leeds Met duo of Alex Walmsley and Jimmy Keinhorst. Another from the same prolific institution, Mufaro Mvududu, is playing for Featherstone Rovers.

If you were to ask a slightly different question, though, you might get a radically different answer. Who was the most eminent person and most outstanding future achiever to play rugby league whilst he was a student? I'd take a lot of convincing that the only acceptable answer to that is not David Storey, the author of *This Sporting Life* and of the screenplay that turned his novel into what many consider the best film about sport ever made.

Like Neil Tunnicliffe, Storey went to the Queen Elizabeth Grammar School in Wakefield and from there to the Slade School of Fine Art in London. So far, so moderately unusual in the early 50s. Where Storey - and ultimately his output - is unique lies in how he financed his studies. Away from the rarified artistic atmosphere of the Slade, he earned his crust from a variety of jobs - farm labouring, erecting showground tents, teaching and playing rugby league for Leeds 'A' team. He never made the first team, but for four years he shuttled between art school in Bloomsbury and the school of hard knocks at Headingley. In both settings, he was regarded as something of a freak. At the Slade, he told James Campbell in a profile in the *Guardian* in 2004, he was seen 'as a bit of an oaf.' At Leeds, he was treated as a posh bloke from London, to whom you would only pass the ball if it had a hospital appointment attached to it. You can see where he got his rather jaundiced view of the game, which informs but does not ruin *This Sporting Life*. In both his lives at the time, Storey was the outsider.

'I only really felt at home on the train, where the two different parts of my life came together,' he told Campbell. It was also on the train that he did his writing, much of it concerned with this issue of 'otherness.' It's a feeling that many of us have had, but not many of us turn it into best-selling art or literature. That 'A'-team pay packet he used to collect from the office at Headingley doesn't seem such a bad deal now, because it was only part of the reward.

20. Mathematics:
The Numbers Game and
the Saddest Scoreline in Rugby League

Cynics might claim that rugby league in universities and colleges remains small beer. Fair enough, its numbers trail behind those for football and rugby union, although it compares favourably with a long-established sport like cricket. There are 16 sports organised into leagues under the aegis of BUCS, involving a total of 4,000 teams, which sounds like a lot until you remember that there are 2.3 million students in the country. So the favourite activity for them, as well as for the rest of the nation, is doing nothing.

Pinning down a precise figure for the number of participants in student rugby league since the first stirrings almost half a century ago is fiendishly difficult. I have heard estimates as high as 100,000, but that is little more than a nice, round number. Who better to try to calculate a more realistic figure than the man who started it all, Andrew Cudbertson?

With the help of data supplied by Simon Adamson, he has made some educated guesses.

As a starting point, he has established that at least 91 seats of learning have played competitive rugby league at some stage, ranging from an unbroken 47 years at Leeds to a single season at the likes of Glasgow University and Doncaster College. Many have started, stopped and started again, whilst others have changed their names so often that it can be difficult to follow their trail. For instance, the often successful outpost in Cardiff, has been variously known as South Glamorgan Institute of Higher Education, Cardiff Institute of Higher Education, UWIC and Cardiff Metropolitan University. They are all the same place, as are University College Swansea, University of Wales Swansea and Swansea University. Never let it be said that the higher education sector has not done its best for the British sign-fixing industry, as in: 'They'll all have to come down, Dai. They've changed the name again.'

Then there's the thorny question of 'A'-teams and, occasionally, 'B'-teams and Women's teams. Should they be estimated as having their own pool of players? In the case of the women, definitely; with the others, there's almost certainly some overlapping and doubling up. Cudbertson's spread-sheet is based on a formula that takes account of all this. In a nutshell, he allows for 30 players in a new club's first season, 18 newcomers in the second and 12 each subsequent year after that. 'A' and 'B'-teams give you only an extra eight per season, on the assumption that most of those players will appear somewhere in the first team stats. It might sound a little like inspired guesswork, but, hey, this the man who not only invented student rugby league, but also planned rural bus routes in Oxfordshire - and everyone there got home eventually. According to the Cudbertson Formula, somewhere between 27,000 and 30,000 players have taken part in student rugby league since he and his friends started the ball rolling on Soldiers' Field in Leeds in 1967.

That statistic could be much higher if you include all sorts of disparate groups, from toe-dippers who were arm-twisted into playing part of one match and recoiled in horror, never to go near it again, as well as those who became completely immersed in it and whose lives would be dominated by rugby league from then on. What it would be interesting to know is what proportion of the 30,000 (nice, round number) were from outside the game's traditional reach.

Opinions vary. Hector McNeil, from his experience at Hull, Warwick and the London Skolars, reckons that there has been something like a 50/50 split, which implies 15,000 players involved in rugby league who would not otherwise have had that opportunity. Cudbertson warns, however, that this all depends very much on your vantage point. A club firmly established in the heart of rugby league land, like Leeds Met, for instance, will have a higher proportion of experienced players. On the other hand, a durable but distant operation like Exeter University will have a higher percentage of novices. Typically, they will have two or three experienced players, a few more who have a rough idea and the rest starting from scratch.

Let's assume that Cudbertson's calculations are correct. That would mean there are over 25,000 people out there who played rugby league as students. The current chairman, John Piercy, points to attempts to build up a thriving alumni scene, to enable the SRL to tap into them 'now that they've got a bit of money in their pockets.' There has been some limited success with this, but nothing on a scale to rival rugby union, which sometimes seems to consist primarily of an old boys' network, with everything else added on as an afterthought. For student league, the financial support that can be expected from ex-players is minimal, not least because, as Piercy points out, players for the last few years have been running up debts as quickly as they have been running in the ball.

It costs roughly £200,000 to run the SRL for a season, of which £75,000 comes in the form of a grant from the RFL. That has been the situation since the students' governing body left BARLA 20 years ago, with most of that money going on staff costs. 'The rest of it comes from sponsorship, registration fees and, in the case of tours, from players putting their own hands in their pockets,' says Piercy. From those figures, however, you can have a stab at calculating what it costs to put a new student rugby league player onto the pitch.

Even if the Cudbertson Formula is inexact, it is probably safe to estimate that between 500 and 1,000 new players come into the game every season. If it is closer to the bottom figure, they are costing £400 apiece; if a thousand is more on the mark, they come in at a bargain basement £200 per man. Whether that is cheap or expensive is very much a subjective question. There is nothing with which to compare the price-tag, because no other body brings in that transfusion of new blood every year. Niel Wood suggests that the sum should be done differently. The actual cost to the Rugby League should be factored in at £75,000, he says, because the rest is self-generated. Divide that by the higher number of players he estimates have sampled the game and his league converts come in at a cheap-as-chips £70 apiece. 'And that's without calculating the value of the administrative functions they go on to fill within the game,' he says.

The SRL has enjoyed considerable autonomy in its time as a limited company under the umbrella of League HQ. It might enjoy slightly less in the future, now that it has been re-absorbed into the parent body, as part of the education services section of the RFL's community game department. The main advantage of this that Piercy can see is that it should give access to the League's network of development officers. Unfortunately, it co-incides with what looks like an inevitable cull of some jobs at that level, as the RFL tries to adapt to a reduction in central funding from Sport England. It's the familiar recession equation; you're trying to make more bricks with less straw. It's no wonder that some gaps appear.

Piercy would particularly like to see a proper league in Scotland - a popular item on SRL wish-lists - and he also admits to some embarrassment over student teams sometimes failing to fulfil fixtures in the prestigious Challenge Cup. The problem is easy enough to analyse. Between qualifying for the Cup and actually playing in it, a team can lose all or most of its better players. 'Then they draw a team in London or somewhere and think that there's not much point.'

That leads us, far too neatly, to the question that has troubled mathematicians for millennia: Just what, exactly, is the most depressing score in rugby league?

Let's have a look at some of the obvious candidates. Despite the way those on the receiving end must have felt at the time, it is not one of the record-breaking avalanches like Wigan's 116-0 against Flimby and Fothergill (imagine if they'd only been playing Flimby OR Fothergill), or the 142-4 by which Huddersfield edged out the gallant Blackpool Gladiators in 1994. It is not even the 158 points by which the Student Pioneers abused their hosts' hospitality in Poland. I know from experience that, bitter though it is at the time, this sort of flogging can bind a team together with a perverse pride at surviving it and coming out the other end.

You could make out a better case the following scoreline from September 1984: Hunslet 40 Barrow 41. That hints at depths of frustration that most players can only imagine.

And what about the lonely single point in scores like 40-1, 50-1 and upwards. Not only have you had a stuffing, but somewhere along the line it has seemed worthwhile to drop a goal. That's not so much depressing as poignant and plaintive.

Nil-nil draws have a bad reputation and, in some sports, they deserve one. In rugby league, they can be strangely fascinating; I've seen four and played in one and they are games that you remember. But I would submit that there can only be one choice as The Saddest Score in rugby league - and that is 24-0. Not conventional matches where one side scores four converted tries, you understand, but the 24-nils that are strangled in their infancy and never see the light. Most amateur leagues have this system, where instead of listing Boilermakers' Arms versus Couldn't be Bothered, postponed, they invent four tries and four goals for the side that does turn up, creating an imaginary game with the scoreline Boilermakers' Arms 24 Couldn't be Bothered 0. I remember that, in the Pennine League and the North-West Counties, it used to be 18-0, but that's inflation for you. It also raises the issue of what should happen to games when neither team turns up. Should they be recorded as apparently thrilling 24-all draws?

The point is that, since I started following SRL results with a diligence bordering on the obsessive, there have been rather a lot of 24-nils, each of them a little badge of heartbreak. You can see it all in your mind's eye. The repeated head-count, the desperate phone calls, the crossed out names as someone says that Big Fred was pissed in the students' union bar last night and said he wasn't coming. Finally, the acceptance of the situation and its futility. 'We can't play them with eight men.'

And it's all been a waste of time: that strenuous half-hour training session; the three hours off the beer - all for nothing.

It has to be said that organisers go to great lengths to avoid this scenario. In the lower reaches of the SRL, lending each other players is a way of life, and, although all players are supposed to be registered by BUCS (British University and College Sports), passing strangers still get roped in to make up the numbers. It isn't a problem unique to the students; there are plenty of 24 point (and 18 point) whitewashes in the lower divisions of the amateur game. The trouble is that there aren't enough players to go around. The SRL and BARLA both tend to measure their strength, as any optimists would, at its best point, like a high-water mark on a beach. When the tide goes out - and the availability of lads who play as a hobby ebbs and flows in very much the same way - you're trying to cover the same amount of sand with less water. The 24-nils beckon and, if you have too many of them, you no longer have a team.

All of which makes it the more remarkable that there are so many institutions where rugby league has proved to be not a passing fad, but part of the fabric of the place. It is no exaggeration to say that there are now dozens of universities and colleges at which it would be unthinkable for there not to be at least one rugby league team. Apart from the daddies of the family at Leeds Uni (47 years), there are long unbroken records at Bradford (45 years), Hull (44 years), Lancaster (44 years), Liverpool (46 years), Manchester (45 years), Salford (45 years) and Sheffield (44 years). Oxford have managed 37.

'There are some places we've never cracked and some, like Derby, where we could never get in until the last couple of years,' Piercy says. 'It often just boils down to someone from Castleford or somewhere being very keen to get it going.'

Add together all the seasons that have been played by all the university and college clubs founded since 1966. That's an awful lot of keen lads from Castleford - or, statistically more likely, from Hull. (Is the pioneering spirit stronger, I have to wonder in the light of the number of key movers and shakers from that city, in a place which is on the edge of things and looking outwards? Or are they just reaping the benefits of eating more fish than the rest of us?)

Actually, there is some recent research on this; recent as in the last week before going to press. Russell Murphy, the RFL's data collection officer - yes, they have one of them as well - keeps a register of student players and where they come from. It is not comprehensive, because it relies on students filling in the form, but it currently includes 1,500 names and the breakdown is fascinating.

Split down according to their hometowns, more players come from Leeds than anywhere. Warrington comes second, with Bristol, London, Cardiff and Coventry all figuring strongly. If Cheltenham is bracketed with nearby Gloucester, they are up there with Warrington, which seems to confirm theories about the significance of the South West.

Of students from the heartlands areas, Leeds is the nearest professional club for the largest number, followed by Warrington, Hull, Wigan, York and Huddersfield. The biggest group of all, though, are the 70 per cent of respondents who come from somewhere other than what is generally thought of as home territory for the code. If that is the key finding, then it is also worth noting that London teams draw heavily on the east and south, whilst the North East is dependent to a large degree on in-comers from Yorkshire. One way and another, rugby league is finding its way to participants who, were it not for the SRL, would still be among the uninitiated. At a time when Sport England funding has been squeezed by falling numbers in the game as a whole - and in rugby union and cricket - the spreadsheet provided by Russell and analysed by Andrew Cudbertson tells a more optimistic story.

21. Futurology:
It's Not Rocket Science - It's Trickier Than That

Imagine a Martian landing in the north of England. Not just any old Martian, but one who has developed an obsessive interest in rugby league, thanks to radio waves leaking from what was previously thought to be an uninhabited area of the solar system. Let's say, for the sake of argument, that he arrives in the middle of winter, knocks on the door of Red Hall and asks: 'Take me to your brand leader.' What are we to tell him?

What the extra-terrestrial visitor wants to know is where to go for the best level of rugby league available at that time of the year; personally, I firmly believe that, when the little green men arrive, as one day they surely will, that will be their first priority.

Up until the mid-90s, there would have been no problem; just steer him to the nearest club in the First Division. Even after the Super League revolution, semi-pro rugby league continued to be played in the winter. After that all migrated to summer, the best amateur leagues still played from autumn to spring and we could have sent him there.

Now, though, I would unhesitatingly pack him off to a top-end student game. If he was really lucky, he could have seen Leeds Met draw 6-all with the University of Gloucestershire, in what the Met's coach, Paul Fletcher, called 'a proper game of rugby league.' The Super Six, as that top division is now called, is an unashamedly elite competition. In 2011-2, it was the Super Eight, but a couple of them weren't quite Super enough. 'It's always difficult to know what the right number is,' says John Piercy. 'It's a huge commitment in the amount of travelling involved and it's hard to judge from year to year.' The Super Six is indeed a far-flung, gas-guzzling competition. Apart from Leeds Met and Gloucestershire, it includes Hull, Loughborough, Northumbria and St Mary's in Twickenham. It is not exactly awash with local derbies.

For them, you have to drop down a level, to the three National leagues. In National North, for instance, you have a three-cornered Merseyside rivalry, between the long-established pioneers of Liverpool University, plus Liverpool John Moores and Edge Hill.

If you prefer, National Midlands brings together Nottingham University and Nottingham Trent, whilst National South throws together Oxford and Oxford Brookes.

Down another rung, some of the big guns of the past still lurk. North West 1 is home to Manchester and Salford, as well as Manchester Met. Leeds, for all their long history, are now in the relatively humble setting of the Yorkshire division, which is topped by the city's third university, Leeds Trinity. Fortunes rise and fall; in fact, they can do so rather more quickly in the student game, with its inevitable turn-over of players, than in any other sector of adult rugby league.

The point is that, at all these levels, there are compelling contests to be seen through the British winter; easily good enough to satisfy the most discerning of Martian visitors.

With all due respect to the Pennine League, the North-West Counties (winter), the Hull and District League and the others who have chosen to stick with the old calendar, the cream of amateur open-age rugby league will be played in the summer.

The likelihood is that most of the refusniks will drift in that direction as well. The ones with little choice in the matter are the students. Without a complete restructuring of the academic year - and that seems to be one of the few educational reforms that has not been suggested - or a new Ice Age, the SRL will have to carry on as a winter game. That could be seen as a constraint; the other way of looking at it is as an opportunity. Across great swathes of the country, the best rugby league available will be student games. If you need your rugby fix in winter, the answer is not, as Gary Hetherington once infamously suggested, Leeds Tykes, but Leeds University, Leeds Met or Leeds Trinity. For hard-core leaguies, the SRL almost has the winter months to itself.

That is not to claim that the SRL is poised to become the equivalent of college football in the United States, where in towns and cities without an NFL presence, the student team is the biggest attraction in the place. Somewhere between the custom-built, sold-out stadia of American college sport and the three men and a dog of its British counterpart, however, there is, with suitable promotion, an audience to be had for student rugby league in the winter.

Mind you, it comes with its own built-in problems. I have referred earlier to the amount of use the 3G artificial pitch at Leigh Sporting Village gets from student teams and others. There is an equivalent on the other side of the Pennines at the Leeds Rugby Academy at Kirkstall; it was there - eventually - that I wended my way, towards the end of the research for this book, for a match that showed me just how excellent student rugby league can be.

The Australian Institute of Sport is one of those blue ribband sporting brands that carries with it a guarantee of quality. When the Aussies were beating everyone at everything, the AIS was recognised as one of their main assets, with its ground-breaking cross-disciplinary approach. I was lucky enough 15 years ago to be flown out to see the AIS central operation in Canberra. You could hardly avoid coming away impressed by the concentration of facilities, the pooling of expertise, the cutting edge sports science, the sheer single-minded professionalism of it all. It might look a little less like perfection in the wake of modest Australian performances at the London Olympics, but you would still expect them to have a pretty damn good rugby league team, full of future NRL players and with a sprinkling of potential stars good enough to go on and play Tests.

Surprisingly, they had started their tour with a defeat by France Under-19s - not including Bernard Guilhem, but no doubt featuring several others with full beards and whose passports you would like to see - before walloping the French Under-17s and Wales and being due to face England Students in the big one at Stanningley. I say 'due to' because, travelling across the Pennines to East Leeds with Andrew Cudbertson, we are both wondering about the chances of it being frozen off. Sure enough, the car park at Stanningley is almost empty and a hand-written notice redirects us to Kirkstall, five miles away. It's a bit like taking part in one of those treasure hunts that used to be all the go, but we are behind some hastily-erected barriers on the touchline at the Leeds Rugby Academy in time for the kick-off.

Despite all the messing around and a pitch that makes an ominous clip-clop underfoot, those of us who had followed the clues saw a match well worth hunting down. Australia are as good as you would expect and are threatening to take command, until the England coach, Gareth Pratt, makes a double-substitution. On come Mufaro Mvududu, of Leeds Met and Featherstone Rovers, and Sam Williamson, who, as a Sheffield Hallam student, must be well-placed for a spot of moonlighting with the Eagles. The Aussies - coached by the former Huddersfield star, Brad Drew - can't handle Williamson's destructive running and it looks as though the heavy-weight prop-forward's two tries could decide the game. As so often at so many levels, though, the Australians have just enough class - particularly from half-backs Nathan Wilson and Christian Hazard (signed by Gold Coast and South Sydney respectively) - to win 36-30. A few of the tries are simply brilliant and the whole game is full of controlled aggression and enterprise.

For Andrew, it almost amounts to going full-circle. One of Leeds Uni's first matches, a mere 45 years earlier, had been against Leeds Electricity on their pitch at Kirkstall Power Station nearby; he thinks roughly where McDonalds now stands. They won as well, he remembers, largely thanks to a hat-trick of tries from a winger named Phil Harris, who was pretty raw, as he recalls, but who could shift a bit.

Apart from their geographic proximity, the two matches have little in common. 'The standard has improved so much,' he admits, 'that it's unrecognisable.'

Apart from the overall quality of the play, the memory I shall treasure is of an elderly couple desperately looking for a programme, because their grandson was playing and they were keeping his scrapbook up to date. 'He's a class act, your grandson, on and off the field,' said the RFL's Jim Shuttleworth, the man in charge of said programmes. I don't know what effect it had on the grandparents, but I had a lump in my throat as the teams drifted back to Stanningley for the après-match; improvising and adapting to the last.

The England team no doubt learned much of use to them, ahead of the UK-based 2012 Student World Cup. And beyond that? Although theoretically outside the terms of reference for this book, it is hardly possible to survey the prospects for the future without looking at the Under-19s College League. This is a different beast from the 12 divisions of the SRL proper, consisting of what used to be, and sometimes still are, called Sixth Form Colleges. There are 30 of them, split into five leagues; unlike the SRL, they are concentrated more or less exclusively in the North of England. They include some familiar names: St Helens College; Calderdale; Warrington Collegiate, Ray French's old outfit at Cowley. Slightly different in conception is the Wigan Warriors Educational Academy, which is earmarked to have a sister institution in South Wales.

Given that many college teams rely on the enthusiasm of one member of staff, it is inevitable that they will come and go. As John Piercy points out, they do not have the option that some university and college sides take by essentially running themselves, because they have to have an adult organiser. That goes a long way to explaining why, in general, the Under-19s' competition does not break far out of the famous M62 corridor. What it does have, however, is plenty of emerging talent.

Already, senior clubs like Leeds Met are scouting Under-19s' matches; it is the logical place to look for young men who have the ability and inclination to further their academic and sporting careers in tandem.

22. Final Examination:
Rugby League Needs Students More Than Students Need Rugby League. Discuss.

Saying that student rugby league is at the crossroads is a little like saying that the game as a whole is in crisis. It was, is and probably always will be.

Let's be honest about it. When further education was the preserve of a privileged few per cent, it didn't matter all that much to rugby league whether it had a dialogue with that minority or not. It was nice to have some educated types on the pitch or in the boardroom, but that was as far as it went. When successive governments aspire to putting 50 per cent of young people through further education - even if that is partly motivated by a desire to keep the unemployment figures down - the goal-posts have moved. You can't afford to lose contact with half your potential players, not to mention all the ones who might go into administration, or simply become better-informed and committed spectators.

That is a straightforward enough argument for rugby

league needing students, but one thing that has come through loud and clear in the research for this history is how enriched generations of students have been by their contact with the game.

Yes, it has been a struggle at times, especially when plenty of enemies would have cheerfully throttled the infant at birth, but that has been part of the fun.

Sometimes the bizarre relationship between the two codes of rugby has led to situations which were nothing short of surreal. David Rothery was a student at Huddersfield Technical College in the late 70s. I'll let him tell the story, which I've been saving up like a late substitute shuffling impatiently on the bench in a Cup-tie.

'I was a mad Fartown fan and wanted to get a team going at the tech. I managed to coax, bully and mither a dozen or so other students to get involved and we got the money together to buy a set of shirts. I knew someone who worked at Mitre Sports and he got a couple of balls for us. We were off.

'We played friendly fixtures against BARLA teams during the 78/9 and 79/80 seasons, on Sunday mornings. We had no home ground but used a field at Highfields to train. There were posts but no changing facilities. Our only ever victory came there against Greenhead College, who we beat 40 - 34 [3 point tries and all!]

'Almost all our games were away from home, against open-age clubs like Sailors Home, Birkenshaw and Sharlston Rovers. All open-age teams and quite good ones. We couldn't see the point of playing teams we might actually beat! We were all aged between 16 and 20.

'I remember once burrowing over for a try against Britannia Works from The Pennine League and hearing their captain say "These c…s are going to beat us." We didn't, we lost 24 - 15 in the end, but we rattled them, that's for sure.

'Early in 1980 the Students Union passed a letter to us. It was an invitation from the RFU for interested student teams to take part in an Easter 7s festival to be played at London Irish and sponsored by Grand Met Hotels. Participating teams were to meet their own travelling expenses but accommodation would be provided.

'At first we laughed, but then thought "why not?" So we accepted the invitation even though only one of our team had ever played union. He was a Scottish lad called Hughie Black. The RFU never once asked what code we played! A week before the event we were informed that we had been drawn in a group with Loughborough University, Strathclyde University and The Dublin College of Catering. We set our sights on beating the latter.

'We arrived in London and were picked up by coach at Kings Cross. We were taken to The Piccadilly Hotel and ferried to Sudbury each morning. We couldn't believe how we were being looked after, but were wondering what would happen when they sussed that we were a league team.

'When we arrived at the ground we were really confident that we would turn the Irish catering students over, only to be told that they'd pulled out. Great, 18 - 0 for a forfeit, right! Wrong, London Irish under 21s were playing instead!! On average I would say we were two years younger than the teams we were playing, at a game we'd never played before. We lost all three games, didn't score a point, and I think they finally sussed us after we had been pulled up about four times for not releasing the ball!

'The funniest thing was at the presentation dinner at The Piccadilly. The MC was the ITV boxing commentator Reg Gutteridge and he was pretty funny. He made us the butt of several jokes because we were wooden spoonists and he wondered at one point if we had tried our hand at rugby league, being from Yorkshire. Now Hughie Black, the Scottish lad, had not fully understood what it meant to be a league team in union circles in those days and shouted out 'We *are* a fucking rugby league team.' The look on the face of the RFU official was priceless. We just supped up the free champagne, didn't bother waiting for the cheese and biscuits and headed off into Soho.

'At the height of rugby union's cold war with league there were a bunch of league playing students being wined and dined by Twickers. That was the last time we played together as a team. It was April and most of us were heading off to university the following September. A couple of the lads signed up for St Josephs, but I didn't stay in touch with any of them. We had played 34 fixtures over two years. I doubt that student teams get so many games in today.'

And I doubt whether many of them have a weirder story to relate, so I seriously considered ending the book on that note. As it was, it got edged out by the story of Exeter University student Alex Rembridge. He won the Andrew Cudbertson Spirit of SRL award in 2012, despite the inconvenient detail that he had not actually played a game for them in his two years there. Alex, who got a taste for the game when his school in West London had a crack at a knock-out competition, has had wretched luck with injuries from the first week he arrived at Exeter. So, instead of playing, he has thrown his energies into organising the club, hardly missing a match or a training session. He has run an intra-mural touch competition within the university and has become involved with the local amateur club, the Exeter Centurions. He has even managed to get onto the field for them, but his big moment will be when he makes his debut for the university in his third and final year.

He was at Wrexham during the Student Four Nations to pick up the award with his dad, and all we can do is wish him good luck. I could have closed with a dedication to him, as the representative of the thousands who have played the game at scores of universities and colleges, especially of those for whom it has not always gone entirely smoothly.

A browse through the 1997 SRL brochure, published by the Birmingham-based *Sunday Mercury*, presumably on the grounds that Cheltenham, scene of one of the Ashes Tests, was not too far away, revealed what might be a spiritual cousin. An uncredited article pays tribute to one Dane Vellander of Leeds University's 'B' team. 'Dane rarely escaped the third team, but when one considers that his performance in his early attempts proved that he could neither pass nor tackle, nor catch nor retain possession, it is wonderful to report that he played 21 games for the club, eventually forcing his way into the second team squad on merit. Passing the ball may remain an arcane mystery to him, but he has managed to become a player who utilises his abilities to the full for his team. He reminded his coaches that attitude is the foundation of a good player.'

I'd happily pick him, not only for one symbolic first-team game, but also as a representative of the thousands who have passed through student rugby. In the end, though, I looked closer to home, to my youngest daughter, Sophie, recently graduated from Lincoln. (Any job offers via me). She was on the train back to university when she heard a fellow-student, one she didn't know, telling a mate about his first year there. Because she has investigative reporting in her DNA, or at least a degree in nosiness, she earwigged the conversation and recounted it to me later.

'The main thing has been getting in the rugby team,' he said. 'Not the rugby union. They're a bit up themselves. But in the rugby league club, we have a great time.'

I can't improve on that. End of lecture.

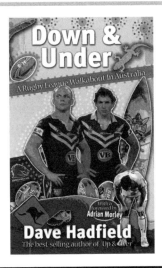
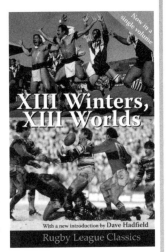

Stay up to date with all our latest releases at
www.scratchingshedpublishing.co.uk